THE BUSINESS BATON

HOW TO SOLVE THE OWNER'S DILEMMA AND EXIT WITH CLARITY AND CONFIDENCE

THE BUSINESS BATON

HOW TO SOLVE THE OWNER'S DILEMMA AND EXIT WITH CLARITY AND CONFIDENCE

GREG HEERES

abundance
collective

Printed in the United States of America

Published by Abundance Collective
Powell, OH

LCCN: 2024911789
Paperback ISBN: 978-1-965419-06-9
Hardcover ISBN: 978-1-965419-07-6
e-book ISBN: 978-1-965419-08-3

Available in paperback, hardcover, e-book, and audiobook.

Table of Contents

Introduction

Do you enjoy stories of how businesses started, the lessons the owners learned, what made them successful, and how to avoid pitfalls? Whether you're a small business owner or strive to be one, this book will be a valuable resource for you.

Let's begin by taking a closer look at business from the past, present, and future. From differing centuries with start-ups and small to big businesses, we can learn much to assist us as we consider the M&A space of business.

Past

The 1700s were heavily agrarian. Most people in the north worked on farms and were self-sufficient, trading in a nearby town for essential items they didn't make themselves. The southern states evolved to farming on multiple sites, providing multi-products or services. Significant industries were cotton and tobacco.

The 1800s were known for invention and industrial development. With industrialization, people saw opportunity beyond farm life. More people moved to cities, and patents began being filed as people saw the possibilities.

From the late nineteenth century through the early 1900s, the United States officially shifted from a rural, agrarian society to an industrial economy centered in large metropolitan areas, thanks in part to rapid innovative developments and the expansion of the country to the Pacific. During this time, millions of patents were filed, and innovation brought a surge in productivity.

The high demand for goods during World War II brought 17 million new workers into the workforce, and unemployment dropped to 1.2 percent. Big business, specifically in the industrial sector, grew into its own, often getting government contracts. The expansion happened rapidly, seemingly overnight.

With the economic expansion in the 1940s, small businesses emerged and catapulted. They became the staple job market and created opportunities for the middle class. However, mega businesses outpaced them, and big businesses dominated every industry.

Even with the gas shortage and other economic pressures in the 1970s, small businesses maintained an important place in our economic system and saw a 49% bump in startups by the 1980s.

Currently, there are over 35 million small businesses in America. They account for 50% of America's GDP. However, they are the hardest hit during recessions and economic instability.

Since 2015, small business startups have been up 15%, even after the hard-hitting 2008 recession. The five-year survival rate has risen to 50%. Technology has allowed small businesses to thrive and mirror mega businesses.

Here are a few small business startups and key entrepreneurs you might recognize:

1950s: Ray Kroc (McDonalds), Tom Love (Loves Truck Stop)
1960s: Phil Knight (Nike)
1970s: Bill Gates (Microsoft), Steve Jobs (Apple)
1980s: Warren Buffet (Berkshire Hathaway), Oprah Winfrey (TV talk show host), Mark Cuban (MicroSolutions)
1990s: Mark Zuckerberg (Facebook), Jeff Bezos (Amazon)
2000s: Elon Musk (Tesla), Mark Cuban (Dallas Mavericks - NBA)

Today

75% of all small to medium privately held companies are owned by Baby Boomers—ages 60-80. There will be a lot of transactions in the next two decades. This will cause a flood effect in the M&A marketplace. There are lots of questions and concerns surrounding this flow of businesses to either merge, be acquired, or, at worst, fold.

Only 1/3 of family-owned businesses will transfer successfully from generation one (G1) to generation two (G2).

About 15% of G3 will successfully transition from G2. These odds are not spectacular.

Future

The importance of selling one's business better will be coming to a head sooner than later. With so much wealth to be realized, the liquidity events will have a massive influence on cash flow, reinvestment, and economic transfer of wealth more than ever seen before.

The importance of succession planning has reached epic proportions. For business owners, you will face quite the dilemma of how to transition both ownership and leadership in order to maintain the company's health and well-being as well as avoid the dreaded capital gains taxes and any government overreach to grab as much liquidity as possible from you.

Here are five M&A trends to look for (or look out for):

1. Lower inflation rates and market stability will definitely stir the pot and light a fire under opportunities.
2. Lower interest rates can stabilize interested parties.
3. A better lending environment will improve business opportunities.
4. Anti-Trust agencies are taking a harder look at businesses buying and selling.
5. New legislation will make a push for M&A deals, and the SEC is coming after crypto.

How do we best deal with the above trends? A solid M&A team is the very first step. Good team advice will be so important for business owners who have either started up a company, bought and grew a company, or turned a company around.

My desire for this book is to equip business owners with sound advice and to warn them of the possible pitfalls of selling one's company.

Ready! Set! Let's Go!

CHAPTER 1

ILL-Prepared

Preparation: the process or action of making something ready for an opportunity.

For many people in life and leadership, being prepared is critical to leading and serving well. Being ill-prepared causes many people to panic, sweat with anxiety, and even make poor decisions because of a reactionary environment.

Being ill-prepared to transition and sell your business could lead to panic, sweat, and poor decision-making. Before we dive into the ill-prepared dilemma, let's build out how businesses are birthed and managed.

Poor planning leads to poor results

Six Traits of Successful Entrepreneurs

Starting and building a business is thrilling and nerve-racking and requires a very specific mindset—an entrepreneurial spirit.

Successful entrepreneurs usually have the following characteristics in abundance.

1. **Robust Work Ethic:** First to arrive. Last to leave. Weekends and holidays as well. Work is always on their mind.

2. **Deep Passion:** Passion and work ethic go hand in hand. Passion helps to ignite and remain motivated. Work ethic enables the business to be strong. Passion is choosing to do what you love.

3. **Creativity:** Thriving new companies are often built on wild creativity. Today's marketplace is aggressive and has a do-or-die competition mentality. Ideas must be original and differentiated from the rest of the industry. Most entrepreneurs consider the possibility that the traditional business solution isn't good enough and are willing to experiment with different creative ideas.

4. **Motivated Self-Starters:** They don't settle for an ordinary job or give up at the first glimpse of difficulty. They do whatever it takes and don't have to be asked or reminded. As a leader, they can't be afraid of failure as they make the difficult decisions regarding the trajectory of their business.

5. **Easygoing Attitude:** Many entrepreneurs will admit that what they thought of starting and what they ended up with turned out much differently than planned. Adaptability is a key. They aren't stuck on the plan or outcome. They easily shake off interruptions or changes and go with the flow since their passion flows.

6. **Eager to Learn:** As we have been told most of our lives and have learned personally, no one knows everything. Being a Jack of All Trades isn't a deterrent for entrepreneurs. They are well-rounded because, when starting a company, they don't have all the funding or the staffing and have to rely on their ability to learn how to get things done.

Turnaround Business Leaders

A turnaround business is a company that's poorly performing financially and stabilizing it with the hope of improvement. But turning around a company isn't as easy as it looks.

Turnaround business leaders are quite different from entrepreneurs in how they see things, what talent sets are needed, and their execution of business skills.

There are five distinct traits of turnaround execs.

1. Restructuring-Minded

If the business is floundering, restructuring may be just what the "doctor" orders. It isn't tossing away the good things, rather finding different ways to scale and improve a companies performance both short term and long term.

2. Patient in the Time-Consuming Process

One way turnaround leaders find success is having the patience in the process. Asking questions. Listening to and testing those responses. Applying what was shared and learned to steadfast knowledge and wisdom from earlier success.

3. In-Depth Planning

I have been around people who don't plan. Often, they live by the seat of their pants. Off the cuff. Reactive. This isn't me, and it certainly isn't the M&A world either.

On the other hand, my best friend is an amazing planner. I will tease them about the pre-pre-pre-planning they do. Honestly, it takes a lot of stress and miscommunication out of the equation. One would be wise to pre-pre-plan when preparing to sell one's company.

I worked with a client who was very intelligent and accomplished. They were gifted with an incredible memory. Their disposition was welcoming. Staff relished this leader's style . . . except they were a bit disheveled and unorganized. When meeting with them at their office, they would swiftly reshuffle their files, coffee cups, and writing instruments so their desk and office environment was more orderly.

Buyers can sense a disorganized person. This doesn't kill the deal, but it certainly can restrict the level of excitement if the seller senses a haphazard and muddled business environment. When I advised an insurance broker on their sale, we actually went around and decluttered all of the offices, conference rooms, and public areas. This really left a good first impression.

4. Resources Used Efficiently

With the future in sight, resources may need to be reallocated where operations are deficient and down. Stewardship of resources is one of the turnaround leaders most critical tasks. Efficiency will be a shot in the arm for a struggling organization.

5. Capital Intense with Regular Metrics

Investing back into the business is the ultimate goal. The process will identify where and when to bolster a department or division or product or service or territory. Metrics are really helpful in a turnaround opportunity because the feedback confirms or redirects capital and resources where it makes the most sense post the process.

*　*　*

Now that we've defined successful entrepreneurs and turn-around business leaders, it's time to explore the consequences of being ill-prepared.

What Disturbances Affect ILL-Prepared?

There are a lot of things out of your control that can affect your business trajectory and traction. Marketplace disruption is a common one. This can be a consolidation of the marketplace, governmental regulations in your industry, or new technology that replaced a current business product or model.

Another disturbance could be a lack of a bullpen (i.e., the next leaders and key staffing). Economic changes affect the bullpen. A poor reputation of one's culture or a financial crisis can affect the bullpen.

Although there are a lot of external factors that can negatively affect your business if you're ill-prepared, my primary focus for business disturbance is a health crisis for the owner. Unfortunately, there isn't a crystal ball to predict who and when something horrible might happen. I tend not to think of the worst, but reality has proven me wrong. Bad things can happen even to good people.

The example I will share is a local business leader I knew fairly well who ran a profitable insurance company with a bright future. He rarely took a vacation, worked 60–70 hours a week, and provided his company a runway when he would taper off and eventually retire. Unfortunately, he never made it to retirement—he died of a massive heartache before he could enjoy the fruits of his labor. This threw the company into a chaotic tailspin. In his wake was a lot of unfinished business, no succession plan, and a leadership cavity. It took a long time for the company to eventually rebound.

My dad advised me to enjoy the business journey. He retired at 58. He got to travel with my mom when they were still young enough to see the world, and I mean really see the world. The insurance company owner cited above never got to do that.

My dad also advised me to set money aside for a rainy day fund. Just in case things go sideways. Basically, my dad was saying to plan but be ready to exit if you need to and have money aside for your exit.

Dilemma Maxim

Being prepared can ease the stress of selling your business and anticipate the challenges you will face when readying your company for ownership transition.

$$$

Liquidity Dilemma Statistic

Did you know that 75 percent of business owners in the M&A space firmly believe that being disorganized leads to productivity loss and profitability lag?[1]

$$$

Case Study: Acme Paper and Office Supply Company

Two brothers started a paper/office supply company during the Great Depression. They faced hard work, sacrifice, reinvestment, and hunger to be successful. Scrimping, resourcefulness, and being open to anything to make them some extra cash kept them going. Using a hands-on approach, the brothers developed a loyal customer base with in-person visits multiple times a week. Titles meant nothing to them. Like most of their generation, a nine-to-five day didn't exist. Yes, they missed payroll a time or two, and they had to refinance and secure double mortgages. They were hustlers, honest, and happy to have a job and provide employment to others.

The business grew incrementally, and the men learned as they went. They lacked an MBA and prestigious pedigree. However, they surrounded themselves with good people in their neighborhood and church. People started to inquire about how to get a better job with them. New employees moved from feeling stagnant or bored to a Paper and Office Supply company that was exciting, in the news, growing, earning more money, and doing well.

Here are a few traits of what this company stood for:

- Put in an honest day's work.
- Pack a lunch, bring it to work, and eat together.
- Serve your customers so well that the competition doesn't have a chance.
- Don't spend more than you make.
- Blood, sweat, and tears are the signs of success.

These two brothers worked well together. They complimented each other's strengths and interests. They were on the same page. They were disciplined and well thought out. They were good at planning and being prepared.

Fast forward 25 years . . .

The families grew and added two sons. It was assumed the kids would join the family business and take over. Similar to farmers, carpenters, and other family businesses during that era.

The two sons worked for their dads. They all got along well. However, the two younger men were quite different from each other. One enjoyed the business. One enjoyed the benefits of the business.

This developed into a slight family situation. The dads felt the pride of starting a company and successfully growing it. The sons joined the family business, working part-time when they were fourteen. One son desired to go to college. The other son spent his free time skateboarding and skiing, both water and snow.

After the younger men worked in the business for about fifteen years, gaining cross-functional experience in all departments, the dads gave their sons an affordable and convenient option to buy them out over time.

Sure, there were a few typical wrinkles to work out. The sons appreciated the opportunity their fathers had gifted them. The dads could have given them the company; however, they knew if the sons had earned the business like they had to, it would increase their chances of success. Helping the sons and teaching them the art of owning a business was a balancing act.

About halfway through the purchase, competition disrupted this father-son business. An office supply conglomerate entered the regional market. The dads prided themselves on offering "made in the USA" products. They loved their country. In fact, both dads served in the military with honors.

The conglomerate bought products and supplies from China, India, and Europe. Price gouging ensued.

The dads and sons were at a precipice. Do they directly compete with the competition and change who they are, or continue as is and trust the loyalty of their customers and their successful plan?

The sons became reactive. Rather than planning or preparing, they made some decisions that put them on a slippery slope. Customers started to barter. One large customer moved to the conglomerate. The value of the American-made and homegrown business became tarnished because the sons hadn't faced adversity like their dads and didn't stay true to the company's values and roots. They were unprepared.

In the end, the sons paid their dads off. The son who liked to skateboard decided to sell his half to his cousin. When they got the company valued, it came back lower than they assumed. They scrambled. This entrepreneurial business started by their dads was hemorrhaging. Being unprepared drove the company's value down in the marketplace. They ended up selling to another conglomerate. The second generation wasn't prepared to fight for the ideals of their dads' company.

Interview: Meet Vincent Mastrovito

Vincent and I met at an Exit Planning conference. Vincent resides in Northern Michigan, which some would claim to be God's country. He is a learner and teacher. He has a charismatic personality. He is deeply committed to helping business owners grow their businesses and exit with a legacy.

Q. What did you learn about business and life growing up, and from whom?

A. All the elders in my life modeled great business habits. My father ran restaurants. My two uncles ran salons and gas stations, respectively. These men showed me two themes about business and life: if you want to be great at something, you must work hard and remain committed.

Q. What motivates you as a leader?

A. I cherish the business stories I hear and can be a part of. The journey of business is so unique for everyone. I get the distinct privilege of assisting them on the journey and completing their story.

Q. How did you enter the M&A space?

A. As a business advisor, I heard business owners delaying and debating their exit journey, and that intrigued me. So, I started inquiring and participating with business leaders/owners, and here we are!

Q. What advice would you like to provide regarding being prepared to sell one's business?

A. In order to exit well, I have witnessed many owners transition to a CEO mindset, which is the most successful transfer of the business. Instead of having to do everything, the CEO oversees the talent, the system, and the outcome, but from a different perspective. Here is my advice to business owners: be open-minded, embrace clear expectations, and understand that the sooner the exit is, the better.

Q. Finally, entertain us with an interesting story.

A. A case I was working on. The dad (owner) wanted to sell the business to the son. There were apparent differences between the generations represented. With some heated exchanges and varying opinions, the dialogue continued even though it was rough. The dad realized he built the business his way during his era, but the son had different ideas but the same outcome. Dad admitted that his son's way could work, and the deal went through successfully. The dad needed to see the son's leadership commitment as well as ownership competency.

CHAPTER 2

Mirror Mirror on the Wall

A solid realtor will tell you that before you sell your house, get your house ready to sell. Curb appeal in real estate does make a difference. The same goes for selling your business, but you need more than curb appeal. There are many different businesses to buy based on niche, size, longevity, and strength. It can also be a very competitive and complicated marketplace.

The Brothers Grimm's Snow White and the Seven Dwarves is a popular story, albeit very dark and wicked. Most know the storyline: An evil queen jealous of Snow White because the queen's magic mirror said Snow White was the fairest of them all. The mirror didn't lie. The queen didn't like the answer, so she poisoned Snow White with an apple.

For the buyers looking to participate in the M&A space, the mirror doesn't lie, nor does the buyer's due diligence. You can make your business look amazing, but the statistics and stories must match what the "mirror" says.

From a personal survey I conducted with M&A professionals, I learned there are eight key accounting mistakes that can hurt how your business looks in the mirror to potential buyers.

1. Overstate cash flow
2. Inaccurate tracking of income
3. Inaccurate tracking of expenses
4. Payable or receivable concerns
5. A blind eye to fraud
6. Unproven CFO/Controller
7. Mixing personal and business expenditures
8. Ugly tax exposure and liability

Let's develop number five because this applies to an actual case that I am very familiar with. There was a large flooring company that had been a beacon as a business in a large Midwest metropolis. Contractors loved this business. They were very successful over the decades. The founder successfully sold it to the next generation (G2). G2 brought in their people over time, assuming all was legit and running smoothly.

When they became curious about selling to a third party, "schtuff" can hit the fan. A buyer asked for an audit. G2 found out their CFO, a boyhood buddy, was embezzling money and had for twelve years.

The financial amount grew to $2 million, and the buyer quickly shut down the deal. The flooring company had such bad press and couldn't recover from the embezzlement loss that they eventually had a fire sale, and no one felt good about the demise of a good company. Keep an eye on fraud. It can rot your legacy.

What Does the "Mirror" Say About Your Business?

A health and fitness coach once said, "The scale don't lie." Well, the same can be said for the proverbial mirror—it doesn't lie to the buyers. If things don't go quite the way you envisioned, don't be poisonous or evil like the queen. Dim the lights on your vanity and face the mirror. Clean up your company so the buyers see your business's true value.

The "Mirror Mirror on the Wall" reminds us that what we see and what they see matter equally as we move closer to being ready to transition and sell our company in a much more sophisticated buying mindset.

Below are the five steps to ensure the "mirror" tells your customers what you want them to see.

MAXIMIZE
SUCCESSION ADVISORS

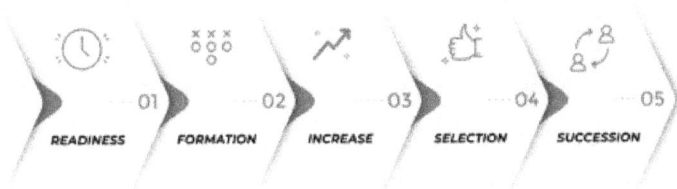

01 READINESS | 02 FORMATION | 03 INCREASE | 04 SELECTION | 05 SUCCESSION

GREG HEERES, Principal Partner
"NAVIGATOR"
616.570.4888 · gregheeres@gmail.com
MaximizeLeadership.com

Readiness

Readiness is my favorite phase, other than the succession phase. It can be divided into these two very important categories:

1. Ownership

First and foremost, the owner(s) must be unified and accept that ownership should be changing hands either internally or externally. Much of the debate in this phase is surrounding the mindset and possibly the hearts of the owner. Are they okay with selling? Do they have an idea of what they will do after the sale and earn out?

I have worked with numerous strong owners who are okay with who they are, what they built, and what they wish to do or become after the sale. I have also worked with others who were not sure. The business was their baby, and they really hadn't thought about what else intrigued them when the time came to sell. These types of owners need to be challenged to think outside their comfort zone and the box at what could be. The business will not be ready to sell until this step is completed.

2. Attraction

Secondly, but equally important, is the business attractive and ready to be analyzed and ideally battled over with numerous vetted offers in the next phases of succession planning?

Areas to focus on to make your business shine to the buyers:

- Clean and maintained facilities
- Sharp staff
- Organized books, folders, and reports
- Informative marketing plan
- Impressive sales reports
- Salesforce and support teams that grade out well
- Confusion-free financials, consistent reporting, and competent

If you have ever worked out at a health club, you have probably witnessed a person or thirteen looking at themselves in the mirrors on the wall of your club. I often asked myself, Why mirrors? Why do you have to look at yourself while exercising and lifting weights?

I heard a leadership speaker share this about mirrors. He said that mirrors are more about self and vanity. A window is more about others and the vitality of life.

We want to create a window in the M&A space where buyers are attracted to your business. A mirror isn't really for the marketplace. It's too often about us.

Formation

Increase

Selection

Succession

Financial Scorecard

EBITDA means earnings before interest, taxes, depreciation, and amortization. A healthy EBITDA is essential to the buyers. This serves the M&A world as a financial scorecard, a consumer's credit report number, or the medical world with your heart rate or cholesterol factor. It's the start of the business valuation. It isn't the end all, but it is often the factor that helps set the range of pricing for the buyer and seller to convene about.

Through the many M&A transactions I have been privy to and honored to be involved with, EBITDA can be very accurate and helpful when deciding to sell and even helpful when deciding to buy a business—I have been on both sides of the table.

Here are a couple of EBITDA mistakes that can be a pitfall for your company:

- Cutting costs by leaving needed positions vacant or by reducing employee benefits like generous health insurance, less contribution to the 401K plan, or unsustainable cuts in marketing and one-time overhead savings.
- Add-backs can be added by assigning responsibilities to owners and top-level leaders without compensation, delaying payment to the commissioned salesforce, or adding back the marketing budget or events or incentive trips after the sale.

A "bad" EBITDA indicates the company is facing operational difficulties and/or is poorly managed. From the M&A buyers market, this will substantially decrease the value of your legacy.

Dilemma Maxim

When you want to catch the attention of a potential romantic partner, it's important to put your best face forward. In the M&A space, this means having all your best ducks in a row.

$$

Liquidity Dilemma Statistic

Did you know that over 50 percent of businesses today don't look their best in the buying M&A marketplace, and it doesn't have to be that way?

$$

Case Study: Acme Financial Planning Services Company

Acme Financial Planning Services started as a boutique firm specializing in a concierge service platform providing financial advice to its customers. Most of the clientele came from a homogenous demographic. For over two decades, they experienced good growth. When they finally merged with another firm and blended the cultures, they had an uptick in revenue.

As the group continued, the advisors aged. Technology wasn't really how they started their boutique, so this wasn't a big investment category in their budget. This became a significant issue for the firm when newer financial planning firms utilizing technology emerged and started dominating the industry. Acme Financial Planning Services began losing clients here and there to these more technologically advanced upstarts. In the beginning, it was negligible. Over time, it started to add up.

A few of the senior partners started to worry. What is their company going to do? What can it do? What should it do? Where will it end up? Does it still have the mojo to remain vibrant and valuable? After soul-searching and prayers, they decided to hire a consultant to right their ship. These consultants came in with guns blazing: paperwork, surveys, findings, and changes. While clients appreciated the re-brand, many staff pushed back because humans are such creatures of habit.

Unfortunately, the uptick expected for the financial firm didn't materialize as they hoped. Discussions began on whether they should sell and how best to be acquired, and that would secure the legacy and, of course, the future of staff and services to their loyal clients.

A valuation was generated on the value of the firm. Initially, the value seemed spot on. The firm's elders felt relieved and giddy that they would get their fair share and earn out. However, as the valuation firm met with each of the partners and leaders, it became apparent that the valuation might need to be tweaked. After some digging, the "Mirror Mirror on the Wall" wasn't as good of a portrait of the company's value. It seemed like the business was aging poorly in the marketplace.

Many of the concerns were not monumental nor unfixable. So, the firm leaders ate some humble pie, took the business off the selling blocks, and did a deep dive into improving. It took time and tears, but they were able to improve the firm's appearance.

The M&A world started to inquire about buying the firm. Healthy competition with differing buyers developed for the firm. The firm's leaders were patient with the offers, though. They followed through on each and provided more info to them. The level of excitement to buy the firm increased weekly.

In the end, they got a very good offer, including security for staff and quality assurances for clients, improved offerings, technology, and reporting. Overall, the acquisition went very well. Everyone was happy. After putting in the work, the Mirror reflected well in the end.

Interview: Meet Jeff York

Jeff was a competitive athlete in high school and college and attended Indiana University Law School and MBA program, graduating with honors. He is well-known in the Midwest as one of the top M&A lawyers and has facilitated and closed many sophisticated and complicated business transactions.

Q. What did you learn about business and life growing up, and from whom?

A. There have been two major contributors to my professional and personal journey: my father and my mentor. They both instilled in me the characteristics that have allowed me to achieve a modicum of success over the years. Here are the characteristics:

- **Follow the "golden rule": treat others how you wish to be treated.** This rule applies to colleagues, staff, opposing counsel, clients, and the maid who cleans the office.
- **Always do your best work, and don't cut corners.** Every client deserves 100% of your effort on each project you are handling.
- **Be responsive.** Don't leave clients hanging and wondering what to expect. Get out in front of all things—good or bad.
- **Treat every referral as if it came from your mother.** You don't want to let your mother down!

Q. What motivates you as a leader?

A. Watching my team progress in their careers and lives (both personally and professionally). As the son of a high school teacher and coach (and former college athlete), everything revolved around sports and teamwork. I learned that personal success, while satisfying, is nothing compared to the feeling of helping others succeed. Every time one of my protégés earns a promotion or a new position, it simply provides me with more motivation to help others.

Q. How did you enter the M&A space?

A. I knew that I wanted to be a business attorney when I was in 8th grade, and I tailored my education around that goal. As I learned more about what exactly that entailed, I was exposed to several M&A transactions (albeit as the ultimate "grunt"). What intrigued me the most about this area of the law was if I paid attention and learned how to do this properly, then my practice could evolve into something that could oftentimes be a "win/win" proposition. If the client can focus on achieving a reasonable result for everyone, we can all walk away from the closing table feeling good about ourselves and the result of our efforts. To the extent I can guide all the players towards that conclusion, I feel like a positive contributor to society.

Q. What advice would you like to share regarding the importance of "Mirror Mirror on the Wall" when selling one's business?

A. "Mirror Mirror on the Wall" is part of the plot of a fairy tale. A crone's mirror would always reply that she was the fairest maiden of all (until a better model came along). The point is that a business owner cannot just surround themselves with advisors who are going to tell them what they want to hear, particularly when selling their business.

Business transition consultants, investment bankers, accountants, and attorneys are some of the independent experts that a business owner needs to rely upon when it is time to sell. Outside board members (even if only an advisory board rather than a fiduciary board) are another avenue to receive objective advice to assist in preparing a company for sale.

Q. Finally, entertain us with an interesting business story.

A. During the late 1990s, I was engaged by a gentleman who was interested in buying a plastic injection molding manufacturer. We put a deal together, and my client operated the company for 15+ years while I acted as outside general counsel for the business.

In the early 2010s, my client was reaching retirement age, and we engaged with an investment banker to find a buyer for the company. Again, we put a deal together with a private equity firm to allow my client to cash out and enjoy his retirement years. A nice, successful run—the result we always strive to achieve.

Several years later, I became outside general counsel and M&A counsel for the business development and acquisition entity controlled by a local Indian tribe. One of the first potential acquisitions we were involved in was a transaction to purchase the same injection molding manufacturer from a private equity firm! What are the odds of my participating in buying the same company twice and selling it once?

CHAPTER 3

——

Truth or Consequences

Back in the 1960s–70s, there was an interesting television quiz show entitled Truth or Consequences. During that time, the host was Bob Barker. The show's storyline was contestants from the audience were given a trivia question to answer, and if they answered wrong, they had to perform a zany, embarrassing stunt in front of a live audience.

As children, we were taught to tell the truth. If we got caught fibbing, then, in some circles, we got our mouths washed out with soap. I preferred Irish Spring soap, but I am admitting nothing.

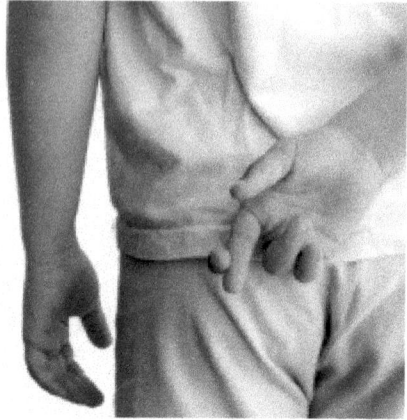

Adults often forget that childhood lesson. The ones most guilty of lying find creative ways to get away with it. I worked with a person who would often say, "To be honest with you." I didn't think much about that initially. Over time, I, along with a few other astute associates, started to question him. We found a few rust spots in his statements, stories, and statistics.

Eventually, we would ask him to clarify or confirm his statement. This irritated him. He would get defensive and louder. His trustworthiness plummeted in a short time. A very sad result for a person who was going to be successful and didn't need to fib to us.

Telling the truth builds lasting trust. Truthfulness is the foundation of human relationships. Truth is the antecedent to trust, and trust is the antecedent to cooperation and getting along at the optimum level/ depth. The absence of truth is unsustainable and impossible for true human interaction.

When you're ready to sell your company, telling the truth is key to ensuring the transaction and transition go well for everyone (buyer, seller, and all the staff).

Benefits of Telling the Truth

If you have raised children, isn't it interesting that if we catch them in a lie, they dig deeper, double down, and deny it? This makes the situation worse. I have asked my kids why they don't just come out and tell the truth. I know it's not peaceful parenting, but a few times I just want to scream, "Just tell the truth!"

Sometimes, kids may simply speak before they think. But often, they will fib because they want to:

1. Try out a new behavior to see what happens
2. Gain approval
3. Appear bigger, better than actuality
4. Move the attention off of themselves
5. Spare someone's feelings

Maybe an adult list of reasons one would not tell the truth would look very similar to the above kids' list. As we grow up, we're supposed to evolve the moral compass to automatically tell the truth. But there are times when people struggle. In those instances, it's important to understand why the truth is better than the lie.

1. You don't have to remember your lies or who you told them to.
2. You will earn trust and respect.
3. You will create deeper connections.
4. You will feel more confident and less doubt.
5. Trust invites more opportunities.
6. Lying takes energy and is draining.
7. You won't be embarrassed by telling the truth like you would if you lied.

8. Truth attracts truth. Like-minded people can accomplish much.
9. You will sleep better.
10. You never have to develop a campaign to clear your name.

Lying is the silver bullet for M&A deals to disintegrate. For example, I know of a business owner in the advertising industry who presented his company as if it were over the moon successful. He seemed to get the attention and energy of investment bankers from all over. Then, they started to dig into the stories, explanations, and data.

In the end, the owner's fibs discredited any M&A opportunity. Sadly, the owner never got to sell his company. He ended up being forced to merge with another firm, and the liquidity and legacy of said advertising company were tarnished and buried.

Exaggerations and Embellishments

Exaggerations and embellishments aren't much better than lies. Having been on the buying side of M&A a number of times, the sense is that someone is exaggerating because their business story isn't as good as the one they promote. Certainly, a business owner will need to present well and with passion. That's much different than "BS-ing" others.

There was a health club owner who pumped up his business success. He always had another shiny object to present. Honesty was just hard for him, I guess. In the end, the club folded because there were other club options for members, and the shiny objects never materialized for the benefit of the club's members.

Dilemma Maxim

Trust the M&A process and your advisors and refrain from fibbing because the marketplace of buyers is astute and lacks forgiveness when it comes to a business transaction.

$$$

Did you know that 2/3 of all businesses that try to sell fall through often because of exaggerations or false data, leading to the buyer bailing?

$$$

Case Study: Acme Multi-Level Marketing Company

Back when "Ma Bell" was broken up by the FCC and other government arms, there was an opportunity to resell long-distance services as independents and as entrepreneurs. Long-distance carriers became a dime a dozen. It looked like the Wild Wild West, with everyone trying to get their hand in the cookie jar.

Acme Multi-Level Marketing firm created enticing recruitment statements to attract employees.

- Easy sale process with cheap costs for phone service.
- Make lots of cash quickly.
- No service requirements for long-distance customers.
- Perpetual income.
- One can quit their day job.

It started well. The company had great momentum with lots of opportunities. The employees were getting attention-grabbing commission checks. Then, the wheels fell off, and the higher-ups scrambled.

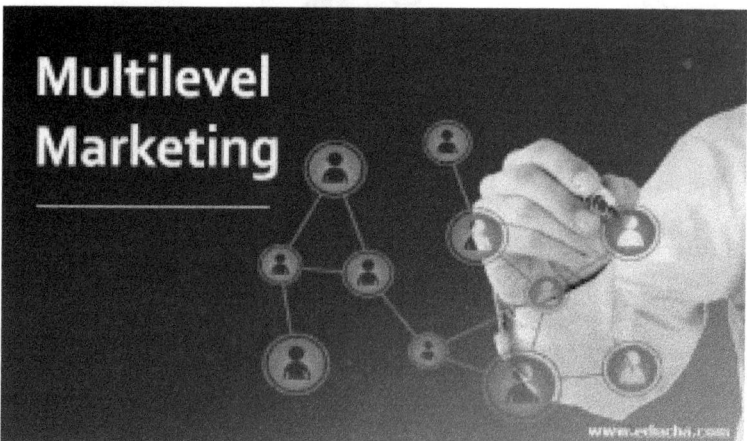

In football, when the quarterback has to scramble, it usually ends with a sack, incomplete pass, or, if lucky, the quarterback safely running out of bounds. In this business, the scrambling concluded with a few embellishments sprinkled with some bad news, and the result was lawsuits and complaints filed.

The embellishments (aka fibs) were from the carriers to the MLM organization without much recourse. People promised things to customers. The customers didn't receive what they needed. Communication was choppy and maybe dishonest. The MLM got hoodwinked by the long-distance carriers. Both ended up not being truthful.

The carriers went their own way and reorganized their sales distribution channels and the founders of the MLM kept their new mansions, yachts, and sports cars. The actual worker bees ended up frustrated with broken promises and dreams.

Interview: Meet Neil Kimball

Neil is one of the most honest, humble, and heroic attorneys in estate planning because he protects his clients from unnecessary stress. He received his undergraduate education and law degree from the University of Arizona and Arizona State University, respectively.

Q. What did you learn about business and life growing up, and from whom?

A. My father taught me about discipline and hard work combined with compassion. The first attorney I worked for was a great mentor who taught me how to communicate with clients in a clear manner and with "plain English" rather than legalese.

Q. What motivates you as a leader?

A. I enjoy developing a practice that seeks to exceed client expectations in an efficient and cost-effective manner. I also enjoy helping clients work through the complexities of business and estate planning issues. They can often be emotionally challenging for the client. If I can simplify things for the client and make their life a bit easier, that is rewarding to me. Essentially, living by the Golden Rule works not only for your relationship with co-workers and friends but also for your business development.

Q. How did you enter the M&A space?

A. I started my practice working almost entirely in business and real estate transactions. Over time, my practice has moved more to estate planning and succession planning for business owners and professionals.

Q. What advice would you like to provide regarding the importance of being truthful when selling one's business?

A. When selling your business, honesty is huge. If you ignore issues important to a buyer, or worse, hide or obfuscate, the deal is likely to fall through either during the due diligence process or afterward through a claim for breach of the representations and warranties that you will undoubtedly have to make in the agreement. Dishonesty will cost you financially and your reputation moving forward.

Q. Finally, entertain us with an interesting business story.

A. I have clients who had owned a business together. Their prior corporate attorney had drafted agreements for their entities that used a formula for valuing their interests in the event of a buyout of a shareholder at death. However, over time and with some changes in their operations, the formula was not updated or tested. When one of the owners died, his heirs were seeking to be paid according to the formula, even though it would have resulted in their being paid an amount equal to about 90 percent of the equity in the business.

The matter settled, but it taught me the danger of using a formula if it is not regularly tested and revised as necessary. Often, an appraisal at the time of a buy-out is better. Agreements should be regularly reviewed to make sure they still fit and make sense for reaching a fair result.

CHAPTER 4

Bad News Bears

Bad News Bears is a film that was originally released in 1976, starring Walter Matthau, and again in 2005, with the lead baseball coach played by Billy Bob Thornton. Thornton was a washed-up minor-league baseball player. He ends up coaching a rag-tag little league team of misfits. Through unconventional and comedic team-building exercises and his odd, at times, coaching style, Thornton takes this hapless team into a contender to play their ultimate rivals, the Yankees. What an epic sports movie and storyline!

If you are a sports fan, you will recognize a short list of fantastic coaches from various sports:

> Basketball - John Wooden
> Football - George Halas
> Baseball - Sparky Anderson
> Hockey - Scotty Bowman

These and many other coaches have influenced, instructed, and inspired their teams to win games and win at life. We can learn a lot from them. Many have written books, quoted with clinkers, and become society's role models.

Team chemistry, competency, and collaboration are often topics of John Wooden. He is quoted saying, "A player who makes a team great is more valuable than a great player. Losing yourself in the group, for the good of the group, that's teamwork."

Relating this to M&A, a good succession plan involves many teammates in their expertise space (navigator, tax, philanthropy, legal, etc). The navigator plays the coach or maybe even the quarterback. They hold the huddles, keep the team united, and keep the owner engaged.

United

It is so important to get the right teammates for your maximum M&A experience and succession. Don't put a rag-tag team together based on how you always worked with them: an attorney is an attorney, or a CPA is a CPA. Based on the experience of many M&A professionals, that assumption is not true.

Ultimately, you want the best of the best and all in the right seat on the business bus and going in the correct direction together for you. Walter Matthau and Billy Bob Thornton would concur if interviewed for this book.

From an HR perspective, most have read or heard, or maybe worse, even experienced, that people leave a job not because of pay but more often because of a poor supervisor. Bad advisors are the same. Most business deals go poorly or crash before succession because of a team of advisors that don't work well together. A sports analogy (football) would be the owner of the business is the owner of the team/franchise. The navigator is the quarterback. The skill positions (the rest of the football team) are filled by top-shelf leaders in their industry (such as wealth managers, attorneys, accountants, bankers, etc.).

If you have an NFL team near where you grew up or live currently, finding a good quarterback is not easy. Many NFL drafts have included selecting a quarterback in the first round to, unfortunately, end up with a bust as a quarterback. Some sports experts have said playing quarterback is the hardest single position in any sport. Goalies in hockey and soccer, catchers in softball and baseball, point guards in basketball, and boleros in volleyball are also difficult to play. When entering the huddle of succession planning toward an M&A deal, keep in mind the importance of contracting with the M&A quarterback.

Tug-O-War

"The Pull" is a collegiate tug-o-war contest at a private, liberal arts college in Holland, MI, called Hope College (also referred to as the Harvard of the Midwest). The Pull started in 1909. It pits the freshmen vs the sophomores. There have been only four ties in over 110 years.

M&A teams can play tug-o-war for power, attention, credit, and the trophy when selling a business to an owner. Compatibility is so important. Unity of mind and heart to serve the business owner.

Dilemma Maxim

Being a successful entrepreneur, inventor, and business person takes a lot. It isn't by chance. It's by character, competence, and capabilities. Running a company takes guts and good decision-making. Selling your company isn't easy, either. Select a dynamite M&A navigator and assemble best-in-practice M&A professionals to get you to the finish line.

$$

Did you know that MLB professional baseball players who hit .300 are considered all-stars? And the NBA's free throw shooting average is 76 percent? Make sure your team is full of all-stars, not average players.

$$

Case Study: Acme Stamp & Wire Company

Post-WWII, many businesses and industries emerged from the war to post-war transition from the war supply and government contracts to a free enterprise marketplace. One large industry that's still going strong is the steel and metal business.

Let me introduce you to a third-generation stamp and wire company in the windy city. To properly get a framework for this case, the founder was a handyman. He wasn't an engineer by education, but he could create, invent, and jerryrig anything. He was God-fearing and hard-working.

He modeled effort and sacrifice to his kids. One of his sons really took a liking to Acme Stamp & Wire and caught on quickly. Willing to skip the roller skating party in middle school to go to work with his dad, a simple, unwritten plan materialized between Generation 1 (G1) and Generation 2 (G2).

After high school, the son took some college courses but really wanted to get back to building, manufacturing, and selling steel and metal goods with his dad. He networked and learned new ways and things to try at Acme Stamp & Wire. The father, however, was content to just keep doing what worked. The slight disagreements grew, and soon, there was a distance between the founder and the heir apparent. But because the father held fast to the saying he frequently said, "Dance with who brung ya," the transition of ownership was accomplished.

Fast-forward a couple of decades, and the son (G2) had two kids (G3) in the business. The G2 couple wanted to get away more and travel while in good health. G2 and G3 began casually discussing selling the company. Of course, the two kids were honored, but they didn't really know how to proceed.

G2 asked a few influential folks in town who could help them plan for a transition of ownership and leadership. They got the name of someone who had done deals (insert Windy City accent from the south side). They called the person, shared what they wanted, and listened to what he would do. They signed a contract, and the business coach began.

When things got dicey between G2 and G3 over some pricing crunches and missed sales goals, the tension spilled over. The coach jumped into the situation to act as a referee. As emotions got higher, facts got skewed, and sides were taken. Things were said that maybe weren't accurate or pleasant.

Frustrated with the increasing tension between the generations, the coach threw up his arms and walked out, leaving the family business shocked. Having a coach quit was discouraging for the goal of selling the company to the kids.

They went back to the drawing board, pretty much discounting what the coach had suggested because of the distaste left for how he quit. In the wake of the failures, the family decided to table the conversation to transfer the business for a period of time.

A few interesting factors developed during the couple of years following that, bringing them back to the family business table. This time, they picked the right team to help with the transition and worked together as a family or a team per se—and it all ended well for G2 and G3.

Interview: Meet Greg Heeres

Greg actually played quarterback and knows the value of having exceptional teammates. Having good advisors is like having teammates who have your back and bring their "A" game to M&A. Greg has bought and sold companies in his career. He studied Marketing and Psychology at Hope College (undergrad), Leadership and Organizational Development at Regent University, and Executive/Strategic Leadership at the University of Miami (graduate).

Q. What did you learn about business and life growing up, and from whom?

A. My parents and grandparents were excellent role models for life and business. I had a number of influential coaches, teachers, and pastors as well. In summary, they all shared a focus on character and less on reputation. Work hard and keep your "nose clean."

Q. What motivates you as a leader?

A. Faith. Family. Friends. And new people not yet acquainted with. Doing the right thing—not the easy thing—for all.

Standing up for what is right takes a spine. Drifting with society doesn't work out.

Q. How did you enter the M&A space?

A. In my career to this point, I have grown companies, acquired companies, and sold companies; an M&A advisor invited me to consider coaching and consulting family-owned businesses, especially navigating the selling of one's company and exiting with a legacy.

Q. What advice would you like to provide regarding a meritorious team of advisors when selling one's business?

A. Good chemistry of an M&A team for the business owner is so critical for the process and eventual positive outcome for the business owner, business, employees, and customers of the business. Good teammates gel together for the good.

Q. Finally, entertain us with an interesting business story.

A. Related to M&A, during a recent M&A advisor agreement I recently engaged with, I interviewed a host of people for the business owner—family and key leaders/managers. I asked them this question: "At the end of this succession journey, what is most important to you?" A number of them in the one-on-one interview/assessment shared they wanted a good Easter and Christmas. I took a step back and thought to myself, The business is one thing. Getting along as a family and workmates was ultimately important versus titles and wages. M&A has an art and science to it. Science is the EBITDA and business value. The art is remaining close, respectful, and engaged with each other in the end.

CHAPTER 5

Expectations + Realization = Frustration

The mental health and correctional industries currently face an onslaught of emotional and mental afflictions. Who hasn't wanted to punch their laptop or slam their telephone down after frustrating news? I worked near a person who went from 0 to 100 mph when things didn't go as expected. Their "Ugh" was loud enough for me to hear them many office doors away.

Self-control lies at the core of many of these explosions. When things don't go as expected, those surface feelings ignite. We witness this everywhere in society. Recently, while watching an NBA game, I saw the refs miss a call. The fouled "star" from the Los Angeles Lakers fell to the court and threw a temper tantrum.

Emotional regulation is vital for business professionals, specifically in Mergers and Acquisitions. Selling one's business can mirror a sporting event. The coach begins with a great game plan but needs to call a timeout once in a while and make adjustments at half-time.

It's important to view the process and opportunity of succession from inside, outside, up, and down. One must see their business and the process of M&A from all angles. With so many moving parts and numerous phases, a clear perspective and reference point greatly alleviate the owner's frustration if the expectations don't meet realization.

Frustration

Frustration commonly follows stress, but it also arises when a goal or expectation is unmet. There are various types of frustration we can experience: personal, conflicting, pressure, and environmental.[2] However, how someone reacts to this frustration varies greatly: Some have short-term reactions to frustration, while others have long-term reactions. The reactions are often not thought through and can leave the person seeing red, among other physical effects like:

- Anger
- Quitting
- Loss of self-esteem
- Depleted self-confidence
- Stress
- Depression

Going into the sale of one's business, one has high hopes and expectations. Frustration teeters on the outcome of many different pieces and people. When things take a turn, all heck can break loose. This can be irreparable.

Having been at the proverbial M&A table with a frustrated owner, this resonates strongly with me. In one such case, a partner in a financial firm lost his cool and was asked to step out of the board room. From the Zoom call, they concurred that he should sit the talks and negotiations out because he was losing his cool. Not being able to control his frustration or reactions to the emotion excluded him from the important details of the transaction.

Realistic

Realists are sometimes criticized for their seemingly neutral views: "The glass isn't half full or half empty. It's holding 50 percent of its potential." In the M&A world, knowing your realistic spot on the spectrum is very beneficial to reaching a win-win deal.

A business owner has to be realistic in many facets of running a company, like knowing variables such as your customers and vendors' pricing changes, sales performance, cost of goods, etc. Realistic leadership is being able to see things as they really are and dealing with them in a practical and sensible way.

When selling a business, a realistic approach is recommended.

A professional suggestion is to agree to "date" the buyer(s) to get the real experience, not the first/best impression. Vet out the offers with a calm, level-headed approach. As my grandpa, who was a good businessman, liked to say: "Don't put lipstick on a pig." In other words, be willing to walk away from a bad deal.

Dilemma Maxim

Escalating emotions in the negotiating portion of succession can ruin a deal and a company's legacy. Have your "walk-away" in mind and lead through the finish line.

$$

Did you know that 1/3 of the general population recently admitted losing their cool over a small or trivial matter? Imagine how many deals there are in the M&A world and how many buyers/sellers get frustrated with deals that fall through or a business that doesn't succeed after ownership changes

$$

Case Study: Acme Logistics Company

I enjoy working with privately held, family-owned businesses. The sacrifices, difficult times, and challenges the pioneers of the business faced prove inspiring. Plus, it takes a strong entrepreneurial spirit to lead a company to success.

Acme Logistics possessed all those attributes. It started with a shoestring budget and an ambition to build something new. The owner learned business lessons along the way and added key personnel to scale growth. Those early team members embraced being good stewards of the business.

Striving to be relevant and establishing best practices led this owner to expand his logistics business and add new companies and services to meet the needs of his customers.

He never faced a dull moment. From staffing, pricing, sales, and raising a family to serving at church and community nonprofit boards, he developed as a leader as well as a small business owner.

His high work ethic carried him to success. Arriving at work early, leaving late, and logging sixty-five hours or more a week was common for this logistics owner.

Acme Logistics was recognized as one of the top ten companies in its industry, often given surveys and opportunities to try new products or systems, and seen as a national leader in excellence.

Things were going well until someone called the owner's health into question. This prompted discussions of selling. Family and key management became afraid the health scare could disrupt expectations and cause frustrations to bubble up because of uncertainty.

The owner invited me in to navigate the process with the family and the management team and to quarterback the succession discussions and decisions. After everyone had an opportunity to feel heard, calmer heads prevailed as they felt reassured about the fairness of the process and the importance of the legacy of the business to the family and the community.

The disruptor definitely put people on high alert. Building the logistics company felt much more rewarding than any plan to hand the business over. Most owners have no issue setting expectations; however, achieving them is not common. Our team gave the company the tools to define the process, engage others, and reach the desired end without losing people or tempers.

This unique case allowed me to see the vast difference between launching a business and leaving a legacy. Managing expectations and accepting the possible realities is important for both the owner and the business.

Interview: Meet Paul Damon

Paul and I have known each other well for decades. He possesses a passion for family businesses, financial planning, and helping leaders excel. Along with his great stature, he has a big heart for people and meaningful causes. He is a fantastic husband and father, as well as a good friend. To top it off, he is tall, dark, and handsome.

Q. What did you learn about business and life growing up, and from whom?

A. I learned the lessons of hard work and dedication from my dad and several mentors I had early in my business career. I saw that if I worked hard, I could accomplish the goals I set for myself. My dad encouraged me to work hard and practice so I can succeed. My dad was always there to practice with me in the backyard or the basement, doing my weight training. I heard John Maxwell say: Try is what we do before we are committed to our goals. Practice is what we do after we commit to our goals. When I went to Hope College to play football, I wanted to be a quarterback, the position I had always played growing up. Truth was, I wasn't that good of a quarterback, but my pride got in the way. My coach, Ray Smith, saw potential in me to be a good tight end. He called me into his office to tell me he was moving me to TE. I was not happy and did not have a good attitude. In fact, I stunk at blocking because I had never had to do it. But I could catch a pass; that was my God-given talent. I had to work hard to be a good tight end. After lots of weight training and blocking practice, I became the leading receiver on the team and was named first-team All-American as a senior. This showed me that if I worked hard and had some talent, I could accomplish a lot. Still, to this day, when I see Ray Smith, he reminds me of that experience and how, at first, I resisted, but once I owned my success, I was able to be successful.

Q. What motivates you as a leader?

A. I am motivated to make a difference. That is what drives me. CANI – Constant And Never-ending Improvement. I want to be someone who is a blessing to others and is always willing to be generous with my time, talent, treasure, and tribe. God created me for a purpose, and I strive to live that out every day.

Q. How did you enter the M&A space?

A. My company, Stewardship Planning Partners, focuses on helping families and non-profits maximize their God-given blessings to make a difference in the world. Our work with families often is because they own a business and want to use their business to make an eternal impact. There are very powerful applications of charitable giving strategies to help them maximize their stewardship impact. We work with non-profits to help them partner with families to be a conduit to use all their God-given resources to change the world. I love the work we get to do and how we can positively impact families and non-profits to make the world a better place and to know and make known our amazing God.

Q. What advice would you like to provide regarding the frustration that comes with the M&A space when selling one's business?

A. I admit I experience frustration when I have conversations with owners of family businesses, and they are unwilling to consider any philanthropy in their planning. Often, they will receive $10M, $20M, $30M or more when they sell, and they still don't want to give any to charity. The frustration increases because by integrating charitable planning into the sale of the business, they can eliminate a ton of tax and utilize those savings to make significant gifts to wonderful charities that do amazing work. They, in essence, throw away millions of dollars in taxes just to retain a few extra dollars they don't need. Getting to the question of "How much do we need?" is important.

Q. Finally, entertain us with an interesting business story.

A. Not sure how humorous it is, but here is a story that impacted me. I was visiting with a couple who have been long-time clients of mine. Their estate was worth about $8 Million, and they told me they had two sons. I asked them about their estate plan, and they said they wanted to give 50% to each son. None to charity. I said to them, "Is that the right amount?" They looked at each other and then looked back at me. They looked at each other again and back at me. In unison—it almost seemed practiced—they said, "We don't know. We never thought about it!" Wow, a net worth of $8 Million and no thought as to how to allocate that to charity, heirs, and the IRS. I learned a valuable lesson. I want to help others actually think about it and have a God-ordained plan for what to do with everything we steward during our lifetime and after our promotion.

CHAPTER 6

Assumptions

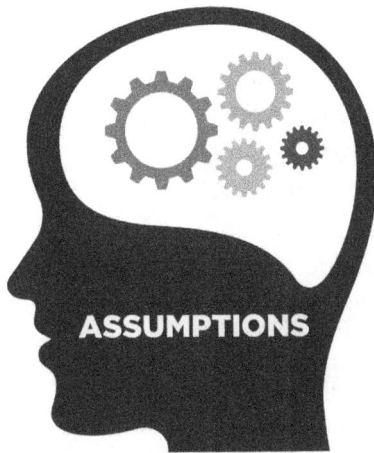

ASSUMPTIONS

In life and business, people make assumptions. They use past factors, tendencies, and average data to make decisions. As we study assumptions and how they relate to mergers and acquisitions, we find the bulk of assumptions fall into the category of opinions or feelings. And while assumptions can create a starting place, they certainly are not the Gospel.

For entertainment as well as education purposes, let's visit ten common life assumptions.

1. Parenting teenagers is a challenge.
2. Spending time with some family members isn't easy.
3. Everyone is eager to retire.
4. If you are busy, you must be productive.
5. Going into debt to live a better life is acceptable.
6. In-laws can be a booger to deal with at times.
7. Money shouldn't change you.
8. Being religious is a sign of weakness and is boring.
9. The terrible twos is legitimate.
10. People probably talk about you behind your back.

An assumption could turn out to be true, but humanity assumes often, easily, and too often incorrectly. Here's a personal example. While vacationing in the Caribbean, someone asked if I was from Miami or Sweden because of my tan and blond hair. I am not from either place. Another example involves my college roommate. He played football and was pretty big. Everyone assumed he planned to work in construction. No one pegged him for a CPA.

In business, assumptions can be costly. For example, I was a partner in a large sales organization where we vetted and hired many young sales guns. One of my partners had a preference for a certain college and a discriminatory position regarding another. As you might have predicted, his favored college just didn't produce the sales hunters we needed, while the colleges he had negative assumptions about supplied us with very good sales professionals and two future partners.

Common Business Assumptions Related to M&A

Profitability and cash flow accuracy are key components to selling your business for the maximum value. Unfortunately, the odds of predicting them correctly are as good as Jed Clampett from the Beverly Hillbillies shooting a rifle and striking oil.

One can look back and create forecasts based on educated assumptions. For buyers, those numbers offer a good indicator, but no one can guarantee the same results going forward.

One education and curriculum company M&A transaction looked exciting from the get-go. The buyer wanted to diversify their marketplace holdings. After all parties did their due diligence, the buyer became hesitant. They knew wrong assumptions could develop into a problem. The buyer and seller negotiated a win-win based on projections—a fancy word for assumptions. The deal worked out but might have stalled indefinitely if the two sides hadn't settled on similar assumptions. Seller and buyer assumptions could have potentially ended up a zillion kilometers apart.

Two other areas of assumption that can make or break a deal are protection and people. Buyers make assumptions based on market and industry trends. A company's best practices can be a wonderfully accurate indicator of performance and possibilities. The buyer wants someone to attest that these practices and the profit they bring will continue—that their investment will be protected, market influences will be defensible, and the industry will remain secure. Obviously, no one can make such promises; however, the seller maximizes value when their company is prepared to make these assumptions as realistic as possible.

Additionally, loyalty and commitment from the current staff are highly important from the buyer's perspective. They do not want a mass exodus if they agree to purchase a business. Sellers should include dialogue and confirm the staff's commitment through the succession planning process. It's a great opportunity to relate to the staff and how important they are.

Inflation

Inflation plays a part in the assumptions of the mergers and acquisition world– and in more than merely a macroeconomic avenue. In the M&A world, an inflated assumption or opinion of business worth can get in the way of receiving the maximum value from the most qualified buyer.

Like new parents who believe they have the cutest children in the whole world, business owners often have a skewed view of their business. After birthing it, raising it, feeding it, and sacrificing for it, business owners see the fruit of their labor as particularly precious and valuable. We have to use caution to ensure we don't allow our idea of value to become inflated when entering the M&A marketplace and discussions.

On the other hand, it is equally detrimental to assume your company doesn't have the maximum value or stop building value when you begin to think about negotiations. People who've been taught to remain humble can easily misuse this trait and underestimate the value and potential of their years of hard work.

The merger and acquisition marketplace can help us understand that neither inflating nor diminishing the value of our businesses will help us maximize our profits. Both high and low assumptions can affect your succession plans and impact the buying public. Often, a happy medium rather than a silly high or underappreciated low can be landed on.

Dilemma Maxim

Be careful of assumptions, whether too high or too low, that will affect your succession planning process and how that impacts the buying public.

$$$

Did you know that assumptions, along with poor communication, bad advice, and cultural differences in the M&A space, dismantle 80 percent of proposed deals every year?

$$$

Case Study: Acme Litho Printing Company

From scribes to Johannes Gutenberg's first commercial press in 1450 to Ben Franklin moving the press into the common industry more than 180 years ago, the printing industry has progressed monumentally—especially since the technological age.

Today, the printing and litho business is everywhere. Full-press litho companies have more technology and equipment than the smaller mom-and-pops. Nonetheless, businesses and even personal lives utilize printing for nearly everything. Birth announcements, wedding invitations and decorations, and garage and real estate signs only begin the list of everyday items people get printed. Churches, sports teams, schools, non-profits, sales organizations, and more all take advantage of digital printing.

The Acme brothers arrived on American soil in the early nineteen hundreds. Their hard work, determination, and knowledge of the Gutenberg and Franklin Press techniques forged Acme Co. Litho within a few years of their immigration.

The company grew organically, allowing it to hire more craftsmen to run the printing equipment. The brothers saw massive changes in the industry–especially about the time the next generation took their places within the company. Fortunately, the forward-thinking pair prepared for the rise in automated printing and the decline in manual labor-heavy production. They discovered niches in news, media, real estate signage, and other printing products.

Expanding beyond their geographic area, they landed big deals in the entertainment industry from California to New York. However, This exciting time for the litho company wasn't without its challenges.

Litho printing high-resolution posters, stands, movie boxes, and other select media requires expensive equipment. Expansion meant the brothers had to reinvest heavily. They borrowed and leveraged to keep the company relevant.

As the third generation came on board, the founders began thinking about retirement. The second generation took the reins, and the brothers proudly watched their grandchildren learn the trade.

A big part of the brothers' success was their ability to make educated and correct assumptions. All businesses must operate on assumptions; however, the growth of Acme Litho meant the brothers had to not only navigate living in a new world but also learn to keep up with new technology and industry relations. Each time they added a new niche, they traveled into uncharted territory.

During the first months of expanding and opening their business to other geographical areas, they had to make assumptions regarding delivery timelines. A different team took on the much different task of using another set of assumptions to price magazines. The variety of entertainment industry contracts and shipping variables pushed them to move to multiple shifts to overcome the added pressure.

One decade after the brothers left the company, a schism developed between Generations two and three. Generation two assumed they would be in charge for another fifteen years. Generation three felt that after one decade of hard labor, they should be moving into top management positions. They saw some of Generation two's decisions as too frugal and careful. Generation three wanted to go after the gusto.

The division became obvious to many people around them. And though the two generations assumed they would remain close-knit and celebrate dozens of Easters and Christmas together as a multi-generation family business, things started to unravel.

The entertainment world expanded globally, and Acme Litho Company didn't have the marketing and sales relationships to take advantage of it. The growth the company experienced in the founders' era could no longer be counted on.

Generation Two felt forced to pass the reins to their children. However, their lack of experience meant spending accelerated, and profits took a nosedive. They couldn't climb out. Staff cuts and selling old equipment for twenty cents on the dollar kept them afloat, but it didn't provide enough cash flow to pursue the big entertainment deals they once enjoyed. Faulty assumptions challenged their future.

Despite assumptions that caused a loss in value, Acme Litho Company remains a viable business. If you asked the second generation what happened to their fathers' business, they would say the value plummeted because they took too many things for granted. Assuming what worked in the past would continue for decades did them in. My grandpa often said, "Be careful not to assume because it could make an A$$ of u and me."

Interview: Meet Jessica Starks

Jessica and I met at an Exit Planning Institute event in Michigan. Jessica has accounting, banking, and M&A experience and has closed dozens of deals that were good for both the business owner and the buyer. She is a team player, and I look forward to working with her again to help businesses.

Q. Share what you learned about business and life growing up and from whom?

A. In high school, I took an accounting class at the school district career center, and I really liked it. From there, I went on to get an accounting degree, and then I worked in banking, where I gained knowledge from really solid managers who helped me develop by teaching and modeling success for me. Before my business broker role, my experience at Huntington Bank gave me two succinct lessons that still apply today: First, I need an opportunity to grow. Second, business can ebb and flow and be ok with the various paces and ups and downs.

Q. What motivates you as a leader?

A. I love helping business owners plan and process. Also, the variety of business owners and stories I get to help keep things very interesting. An entrepreneurial spirit is so exciting to be around. Working with business owners is never boring.

Q. How did you enter the M&A space?

A. The M&A space got my attention through my wonderful professional career and personal interests. My husband and I really enjoyed real estate, and working in that field taught me a great deal about two parties discussing and negotiating. We found business opportunities coming our way because of our real estate activities. I bought a Transworld Business Advisors franchise, and as they say, "The rest is history."

Q. What advice would you like to provide regarding the frustration that comes with the M&A space when selling one's business?

A. When working with business owners, I have heard them say, "I need x amount. ." This can be a challenge in the process of transitioning owners and leadership. Additionally, emotions run rampant in the M&A space at times. One unique deal involved an owner who had an interested party they refused to include in the organized vetting process in hopes of a side deal.. Unfortunately, this strategy didn't help the owner get the best buyer. The reaction of the other buyers when they discovered what had happened was detrimental to the owner's business and value.

Q. Finally, entertain us with an interesting business story.

A. Really, there is a business out there for all needs/services. The most interesting business I sold was a service company that picked up deadstock from farms and disposed of the animals. It was smelly and gross for me to think about, promote and sell. However, we got it sold - there is a buyer out there for all types of businesses!

CHAPTER 7

Keep your eye on the ball

Whether or not a person plays or enjoys watching sports, most understand the analogy of keeping your eye on the ball. From golf to baseball and every sport in between, most misses happen when the player gets distracted and looks away from the ball. This key piece of advice will help you avoid pitfalls when selling your business as well.

In spite of the fact we know we need to keep focused, it's easy to take our eyes off the ball in leadership and business.

- Our to-do lists might not jive with our priorities.
- Priorities appear vague.
- "Busy work" sidetracks us.
- We avoid difficult conversations or situations.
- We do not see movement towards important goals.

Too often, these problems become distractions and lead to what some call quiet quitting. This refers to employees who put no more effort into their jobs than absolutely necessary. A 2023 Gallup survey suggested that more than half the U.S. workforce consists of quiet quitters.[3]

This same phenomenon can affect business owners in the merger and acquisition stage. They get distracted by what life will be like after the sale. Others become like a groom on a wedding day. All the hoopla of the engagement and wedding preparations causes cold feet. They become so anxious about the wedding that they take their eye off the prize—the bride.

A business owner with a great deal of energy invested in his company can become just as anxious when he allows any of those reasons to distract him. When you take your eye off the ball as a business owner, it's easy to run scared out of the church.

Productivity

After extensive studies on productivity in the workplace, human resources organizations and associations agree that the many tools and systems used to gauge a person's productivity and engagement make the measurements less than definitive. Regardless of the official number, we know those who remain engaged in their work produce higher than those who deal with distractions all day.

Productivity is critical to the health of a business; therefore, it's also imperative to the value of your mergers and acquisitions.

- Productivity provides an opportunity to increase output without more inputs.
- Increases profitability.
- Enhances competitiveness.
- Improves work-life balance.
- Drives innovation and growth.

As an owner and leader, people watch your words and actions. Positivity breeds positivity; fun-loving opens doors for your staff to have more fun. They must respond to that. If you are fun, they must respond to that. If you are driven, those who watch you respond accordingly.

Similarly, a pessimistic attitude or low productivity brings out those behaviors in others. And when you have made the decision to transfer ownership–internally, externally, or hybrid), they will watch you even closer. It's vital to stay productive even with a sale pending and remain focused even if you dream of retiring.

This brings us to the myths surrounding retiring. Most, if not all, leaders and owners live lives of passion, drive, and competence. You don't lose those traits by moving into a new phase of life. To some, retiring means you have no passion or oomph. They feel like they have nothing to offer. That is completely false. Selling your company does not make you unimportant.

Dilemma Maxim

One can check out at a grocery store, but it is ill-advised to check out when you are an owner and looking to sell. Continue with your foot on the gas pedal for your company. Keep running it. Keep growing and reinvesting while you plan your sale, transition, and exit.

$$

Over 50 percent of all leaders and workers in
America admitted to coasting at work.
This parallels studies on the decline of
productivity over the past ten years.

$$

Case Study: Acme Agriculture Company

After the war, a capable and competent business guy returned home to a hero's welcome and decided to buy a small farm. After some research, He planted produce that was selling well and bought a pair of livestock that were in the highest demand.

His family grew like his crops. By the time they were twelve, his children were driving trucks on the farm, operating tractors with implements, and tending to the livestock. The family worked well together and accepted their roles in the family business.

Over time, he invested in more land, equipment, and seeds to grow more crops and more in-demand livestock. The farm owner was getting the hang of agriculture. His farm did so well that he received several good offers. He declined for a number of reasons.

- It was too early to retire.
- His kids wanted to stay involved in the business.
- He wasn't interested in retiring to Florida.

He bragged often about his homegrown leadership and did a fantastic job of investing in and developing his family members. His bullpen of possible future partners grew to fruition.

One son, in particular, started to excel. Organized and technologically oriented, this son made wise decisions and kept his eye on expenses. Over the years, his leadership abilities took shape.

By the time this son turned thirty, Acme Farms had produced a nice profit each year and had a following of fiercely loyal customers. The farmer paid off his debt and started dabbling in other ventures and unrelated industries.

As the son took over more and more duties, he and the farmer started talking about selling shares internally over time. The entire family agreed this son would be a good person to replace his father.

Unfortunately, father and son had quite different personalities. The farmer was chill; the son was intense. However, the farmer knew he had a limited supply of internal fuel left to run the farm. Plus, his focus had shifted to other investments and opportunities. His son, on the other hand, was full of jet fuel and enthusiastic to focus on the farm as well as the plans he and his father had made.

So, they began negotiations to transfer the running of the farm to the son. Sadly, they didn't enlist the help of an M&A team. Quickly, dialogue lost momentum and direction, and both sides got a bit persnickety. Discussions stalled. To the outsider, the situation looked implosive.

The son recognized the problem and called a business coach to help navigate the ownership change and mend relations. The coach asked powerful questions, listened carefully, and shared his findings in such a mild-mannered way that neither man felt offended.

The coach made this determination:

- The father is a Boomer. The son is a Gen Xer.
- Though egos were easily bruised, they could heal through coaching.
- Their leadership styles were different, but the character of each man aligned well with the position.
- The two had similar goals.; However, their methods of getting to the finish line seemed like they came from two different playbooks.
- The negotiations needed both sides to show humility and recommitment to the real end game.

Discussions got back on track soon after meeting with the business coach. Details of how and why became less important than the big picture of perpetuating the farm. The father recommitted to helping with the business side of the farm and unraveled his other ventures that distracted him.

At the time of this writing, Acme Farms has successfully transitioned both leadership and ownership. Because both men kept their eyes on the ultimate goal of passing this business down through the generations, they were able to put a mark in the win column.

Interview: Meet Randy Rua

Randy and I met over a dozen years ago. I learned something valuable: everything I got a chance to hang out with this highly intelligent guy. Randy has both accounting and investment banking experience and has built two companies: Rua and Associates and Nuvescor. Randy's firm has celebrated a dozen deals a year over the past decade through using consistency and competency.

Q. Share what you learned about business and life growing up and from whom?

A. My father played a significant role in shaping my values, work ethic, and understanding of life, as well as my philosophy toward business and money management. He helped several large companies start new manufacturing facilities, and I was able to join him on those projects. Marc Clevenger also offered guidance, advice, and insights into various aspects of life. My boss, Marc, at my first job at Prince Corporation of Holland, Michigan, also showed me the ropes of the manufacturing business. Lastly, I learned some things from success, but mistakes taught me more. I lost funding in the DOT.COM era, which taught me humility and resilience.

Q. What motivates you as a leader?

A. I have a passion for treating others with respect and have a drive to create a positive and lasting impact. I love team building and team success. I am honored to have a tenured team of professionals who get along and make good things happen in business and the community.

Q. How did you enter the M&A space?

A. Achieving my MBA from USC Marshall School of Business built the foundation for a solid understanding of business principles, including a focus on Mergers & Acquisitions. In addition to education, I had the privilege to buy two businesses, which allowed me to experience acquisition, merge operations, and oversee the financial aspects. This experience and education sparked my interest in the M&A space.

Q. What advice would you like to provide regarding any possible frustration that comes with the M&A space when selling one's business?

A. Stay resilient even if things don't move along at the speed or direction you would prefer. Assemble a team of professionals to guide you and your business. Communicate often. Remember the end goal. And celebrate in the end when things get wrapped up.

Q. Finally, entertain us with an interesting business story.

A. In the early 2000s, amidst the changing landscape of the automotive industry, Motorcraft Innovations recognized the need for modernization if they wanted to remain relevant and competitive. The company specializes in producing components for traditional internal combustion engines, a sector facing disruption due to the rise of electric vehicles (EVs) and increased environmental concerns.

Instead of succumbing to the challenges, MotorCraft Innovations decided to embrace the shift and reinvent itself. The company's leadership, led by a dynamic CEO named Sarah Martinez, saw an opportunity to transition into manufacturing components for EVs, which were gaining momentum.

Because this Michigan-based manufacturing business kept their eyes on the ball, they were able to establish resilience and adaptability in the face of industry changes. It showcases how visionary leadership, innovation, and a willingness to embrace new technologies can lead to success, even in a sector as traditional as manufacturing.

CHAPTER 8

Rigidity

Have you ever met someone and thought, *Wow, he is a little stiff like a heavily starched dress shirt?* Those kinds of people can be tough to converse with, difficult to get to know, hard to figure out, and too rigid to enjoy any fellowship or networking.

The M&A process can feel that rigidity too. The stiff culture can make the organization appear starched. People don't seem free to develop and dare to make changes. It's a bit robotic. Owners, however, have an influence on the rigidity or fluidity of their business.

In M&A deals, the size and complexity of a business can affect rigidity, especially if the enterprise is made up of multiple companies in multiple states or even countries.

Adaption

Most humans avoid change. Few want to adapt, much less thrive. It takes time and patience to accept and embrace change, as well as adapt to a better form, person, product, or service.

Why is change so difficult for humans?

1. Loss of control
2. Too much uncertainty
3. Sudden decisions/surprises
4. Different isn't reassuring to our habits
5. Embarrassing or loss of reputation
6. Concerns of competence and confidence
7. More work
8. Causes a ripple effect
9. Past issues and resentment
10. The threat change presents may be real

In the midst of M&A, the owner will need to change many things—mindset is the biggest one. They have to adapt a new mindset regarding legacy, their exit plan, and what it means to be a good steward of the liquidity event.

One business owner I worked with had a successful business as well as some real estate he intended to sell. The separate LLCs would make it easy for the owner to sell the business to his family and key managers and find an investor to purchase the real estate.

The owner had a realistic view of the real estate's worth, but the M&A Realtor he chose preferred a more aggressive approach. As the deal progressed, both realtors started getting feisty., Neither the seller's M&A representative nor the potential buyer's realtor would budge, and the deal fell through. It is common for some deals to be adversely affected by M&A professionals. So, it's vital to select wisely.

Positivity

One leadership trait found to be very helpful to the succession planning for your business is positivity. Negativity rarely draws good outcomes. Positivity is contagious. It helps the culture and associates to step up, face change, see the best opportunity, and work productively.

We have all encountered a Negative Ned or Nellie. Quite frankly, they are exhausting. Associates exchange at least a third of their day for a paycheck. With Negative Ned, the work feels more like hard labor.

In M&A discussions, Negative Ned can derail the momentum and turn off any buyer's ambition. A positive attitude can be learned and developed. Here are a few ways to remain positive if you have a slight propensity to be a Negative Ned or Nellie.

- Maintain a gratitude diary.
- Understand that self-care isn't selfish.
- Begin your day with energy.
- Avoid gossip and garbage.
- Listen to and share humor.

Be Ready

Stubbornness is a real threat to everyone's M&A experience. Coming to the conversation prepared with ideas, questions, and scenarios can help those on both sides of the table be open to ways to get the deal done.

Research and experience reveal four common disruptors to the M&A discussion. Those who prepare for the four D's create a smoother experience for all involved.

1. **Dissension** amongst the troops brings the first disruptor. Family, managers, and salespeople may decide to leave and become the competition.
2. **Disease** – The health of the owner or their spouse smacks the business and causes worry and concern.
3. **Divorce** can be a force that creates havoc on M&A and succession planning.
4. **Death** is something one can't plan for. Whether it is the owner or a family member, grief can certainly change a person and a succession plan.

Dilemma Maxim

Plan for perfect. Prepare for imperfect. Expects challenges. Embrace tension. And finally, have a walk-away position in mind if things get out of control and become unhealthy for you and your business.

$$

75 percent of all leaders in America admit they can be hard-headed. This will adversely affect succession planning and transference of ownership and leadership.

$$

Case Study: Acme Salvage Company

The salvage industry is very unique. Someone's trash is another person's fortune. Salvaging vehicles and equipment is not easy work. One must have an eye for parts, pricing, and demand. There isn't a lot of competition, and not every community wants a "junkyard" in their backyard.

Acme Salvage began as a true family-filled and family-run business. They employed not only their kids but also cousins, nephews, and nieces.

They built a thriving salvage company using their skills to find opportunities to buy and sell parts. In fact, Acme Salvage became well known nationally, and members of the family served on the American Salvage Association board.

They had a vast inventory, ideal locations, knowledgeable staff, competitive pricing, and an excellent online shopping and shipping service.

Car restoration enthusiasts around the country buzzed about Acme Salvage and their success. Unsolicited inquiries and offers started to come in.

The entire family felt good about the offers and enjoyed the fact competitors, the M&A world, and even the government gave them some attention.

The offers became so inviting that they couldn't ignore them; however, their interest had nothing to do with Grandpa reaching his seventy-sixth birthday. Rather, the opportunity to make a huge profit and do other things with their lives tempted them. Even though the entire clan received a paycheck from Acme Salvage, they started considering the idea of selling.

As the conversation expanded, egos grew. Take a large family, toss in a hint of arrogance, and the Acme Salvage Company took on the air of a tremendously amazing bomb dot com. After much dialogue, they decided to only entertain the top buyers. They felt like they belonged with the big boys.

The M&A team started to get frustrated; meetings ended up dicey and tension-filled. Their reputation leaked to the marketplace, and the buyer's advisors were put off by the Acme Salvage attitude.

The combination of arrogance and rigidity created a huge whammy for the M&A momentum. No one wanted to work with a business that thought and acted like they were better than others.

Acme Salvage's advisory team scrambled to clean up the reputation and hired a PR firm to put a more positive spin on things. Their attempts were too late. Negotiations ceased, and activity slowed to a screeching halt.

To avoid disenfranchising your business from the M&A world, balance confidence with reasonableness. Plummeting interest and dwindling offers forced the salvage company to consider all bidders. A middle-of-the-road buyer ended up being a perfect fit, but the rigid and difficult family almost ruined the legacy.

Interview: Meet Kurt Nederveld

Kurt and I met through an introduction from another M&A advisor. We got along instantly. He is an insightful, problem-solving, opportunity-knocking financier and a unique lender for deals and projects in North America. He is an entrepreneur but, most importantly, a loving husband, a phenomenal father, and a fierce competitor.

Q. Share what you learned about business and life growing up and from whom?

A. I was privileged to have a number of business mentors. First, my father, Gord, began buying and selling real estate and openly discussed the reasons behind buying and selling, how to add value, etc. Second, books that business leaders suggested to me. I learned leadership and business lessons from both my father and from authors.

Q. What motivates you as a leader?

A. First and foremost, I seek to honor my Lord and Savior, Jesus Christ, in all that I do. Next, I want to show my wife, children, employees, and community the definition of servant leadership. Leadership requires one to grow themselves first and then develop others around you. Leaders can make a big difference. Either positive or negative, so choose wisely.

Q. How did you enter the M&A space?

A. In 2011, I launched a marketing firm named Rainstar Marketing. In 2014, I launched a debt advisory firm named Rainstar Capital Group. Both serve commercial lending and commercial real estate and eventually fund acquisitions of businesses.

Q. What advice would you like to provide related to being rigid and hard-headed when financing and selling one's business?

A. Simply, life is short. Value your business and relationships that matter in the end. Selling one's business is a major accomplishment that few have the opportunity to do. Plus, it is a large wealth builder. I advise finding the best fit. Don't get fixated on a certain dollar amount or what it's supposed to look like. One benefit is the stress relief that your business has a legacy, which continues for others when you sell or retire.

Q. Finally, entertain us with an interesting business story.

A. I enjoy the game of golf. It's a difficult game to master, but the networking benefits are invaluable. I often say yes to golf invites and events because you never know who you may meet or know. An example is when I accepted an invitation from a client to play in an event for a local nonprofit. Our group included a business owner, and we hit it off. After the golf event, we met for dinner, and I discovered they needed funding for their business. I got to golf at a really nice course and gained a client and a friend.

CHAPTER 9

The Devil is in the Details

W here did the "the devil is in the details" saying come from, and what does it mean?

The real origin of this idiom is unclear, but German philosopher and poet Friedrich Wilhelm Nietzsche is credited with saying this in the late 1880s. It was most likely a play on the original phrase, "God is in the details." It refers to the fact things may seem straightforward and simple, but in fact, the grandest project depends on the smallest components, and ignoring these details will likely cause problems.[4]

My kids loved being read to before bedtime. Actually, they liked any activity that would delay closing their eyes and going to sleep.

One book that was a big hit for Alexa, Austin, and Addisen was *I Spy*. The book hides items in very busy scenes. The details and clutter made the odd items tricky to find.

This is similar to M&A. The process of succession and transferring ownership and leadership includes a lot of details and clutter. A thoughtful plan, experience, unified team, and succession clarity will help the business owner find the clues, gather the necessary insight, and solve the perplexing dilemma of selling the company correctly and leaving a thriving legacy.

Details

One of my favorite clothing stores ever was Bachrachs. After college, I needed to buy "big boy clothes" for my first real job—no more joggers and backward hats. I walked into Bachrachs in the mall and started to get cotton mouth, probably because of all the styles, colors, textiles, and patterns–so many details. I entered the store with excitement and found knowledgeable sales clerks ready to help me find the right fit. Big Boy job, here I come!

Human resources experts advise companies to hire slowly and fire quickly.. In the same way, the M&A process moves along with an end goal in mind. It slows when the offers start coming in so it can review and digest the details.

My best friend is amazing in the kitchen. In order to create her delicious goodies, desserts, and naughty snacks, she needs to add the ingredients in the right order and with the right amount. Plus, she has to be patient as the ingredients unite in the oven to form the perfect delicacy. Likewise, selling your company means having a plan and hiring a "chef" (aka quarterback or navigator) for your M&A team and process. To get the best result, we must place the right information into the mix and be patient for the perfect succession.

Fine Print

Have you ever read the side effects or cautions on product labels? They can be scary. Here are three odd fine print warning labels and side effects that really caught my attention, and not for good reasons.

A popular motorhome manufacturer lost a large settlement to a customer who put the motorhome on cruise control and left the driver's chair to make a sandwich, leaving the steering wheel unattended. He crashed, got hurt, and sued and won. Now, the operator's manual says in bold print, "Don't operate this vehicle and leave your driver's seat to make a sandwich."

Drug companies place warnings on their products. Some of the side effects are disgusting. Here is a sample list of one prescription common to Americans. "Hallucinations. Memory loss. Blood clots. Convulsions and seizures. Birth defects. Cancer. Loss of 'you name it.' And gassy bowels or anal seepage." Why would you pop that pill with all of these possibilities?

A large manufacturer of hair dryers was forced to place a warning label on the cords, "Do not take hair dryer in the shower, hot tub, bath, pool, or body of water." You wonder what person tried that.

Hiccups and Trip-ups

When selling your business, growing a bullpen of talent is key. Another key is creating an organization and chart to help everyone understand their value and role. The transition of roles is important. To help the company maintain success, we must be certain the next leader/owner can fill our roles.

Let me share the details of two other business value improvement maneuvers.

1. **Earn Out Provision**: This can prove to be a win-win for the seller and buyer. The buyer can get a bit better price by promising the seller a percentage of the profit if revenue exceeds a pre-determined amount. The dilemma for the seller becomes "a bird in the hand or two in the bush." By going slowly and examining the details, this provision can be a huge factor. Plus, Earn Outs create accountability and keep handshakes intact.

2. **Golden Handcuffs:** This business term indicates financial incentives intended to encourage employees to remain with a company for a stipulated period of time. These handcuffs may maximize your business value for the buyer when they realize that certain key employees have incentives to be loyal to the company even during the transition of ownership and leadership.

Dilemma Maxim

As a business owner, you will need a team of advisors, some of whom may need to be surveyors and excavators, to dig deep into the details of the deal. In concept, an offer may be eye-catching. But be sure you read the fine print. And don't leave any stone unturned.

$$\$$$

In business dealings, it's estimated that 90 percent of all deals have critical enterprise details and data that both parties need to read with a fine-tooth comb before proceeding.

$$\$$$

Case Study: Acme Mechanical Contractor Company

Acme Mechanical Contractor Company started fifty years ago–before computers, cell phones, and fax machines. They used carbon paper to make copies of their contracts and rotary phones with six-foot cords that often got tangled. A Rolodex kept their contacts in alphabetical order.

The founder was very good with his hands, familiar with tools, and could operate heavy equipment for mechanical contracting. With an impressive work ethic, his handshake guaranteed his integrity, and his word was his bond.

His growth-minded son joined him in the business after high school and trade school. He was a chip off the old block. Father and son got along well, which isn't always the case in business.

Business started to roll in. The father-son duo served the community everywhere–on civic boards and volunteering at events. They started to gain word-of-mouth business and went on a hiring splurge. New equipment and more services secured them a strong marketplace position.

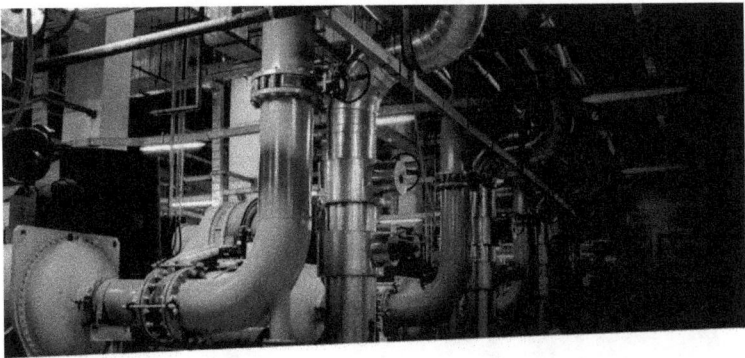

When technology made its entrance into the business world, they adapted. Both men became savvy in communications, cost management, and customer care.

The father eventually declined in health and needed to step away from his lifelong family business. The son's mind and heart were conflicted about the dad's health and his opportunity to buy the business from his parents. The father-son duo worked to find a fair estimate for the value of the business. They decided on the best financial mechanisms and contemplated the most efficient transition.

The father passed away within twenty-four months, but the mechanical company increased its sales, services, and brand. Within five years, the business had impressively doubled. The company's award-winning products and services earned them record-breaking contracts. All was going well. And then . . .

Acme's staff started to retire or leave. Mechanical contractors from outside the region started to give them competition. Pricing got skinny, and their marketplace position weakened. As the son aged, his drive for growth and energy level lessened. It became difficult to maintain that competitive edge.

The son considered selling to his own kids over time. He even planned on discounting the share value for them.

I'm not sure why the son didn't hire an M&A team to work through the details of the business sale. Maybe they didn't know anyone or didn't want to share their business info with strangers. They might have figured that since it was family, they could work through the complex transaction.

Very quickly, the "wheels fell off" the internal sale idea. Hard reality meetings occurred within the family and the company. Even outside vendors and customers got involved. Finally, they secured an M&A "quarterback" to help navigate the journey from readiness to succession.

Unfortunately, the marketplace kept moving and seemed to stay one step ahead of Acme Mechanical. Value started to decline, and the brand wasn't held in the same esteem.

The owner got worn out from trying to jump-start the incline of sales and keep the family together. He often was a contractor by day and a counselor by night.

The M&A team worked diligently to get the company ready to vet buyers so they could get the best offer and partnership going forward. However, by this time in the juncture, it wasn't easy to create interest. The offers were not great, but what else could the team do? The seller was done, tired, and tapped out.

As they sorted through the offers and terms, several common problems arose in the evaluation of offers.

- Family members' roles
- Earn out was too ambitious
- Contingencies ended up being costly
- Excitement in transferring the business legacy lost air

In the end, they accepted an offer with details that weren't easy to swallow for the son of the founder. He expressed guilt about letting his father down.

Interview: Meet Jerry Broekhuis

Jerry and I met on a formidable team of M&A advisors for a mutual client who wished to transition leadership and ownership. Jerry's style is a perfect fit--informative, cautious, thorough, and compatible with other advisors to act in the client's best interest.

Q. Share what you learned about business and life growing up and from whom?

A. I grew up on a small farm, somewhat oblivious to the business aspects of the farm. Being on a farm taught me work was a necessary part of life. My primary teachers were my parents. I had a teacher in high school who invested in real estate both as a rental and also to fix up and flip. My parents taught me debt was bad, but this person showed me the power of leverage. On a complete whim, I took accounting my senior year and absolutely fell in love with it. That class opened my mind to what the business world was about.

Q. What motivates you as a leader?

A. My primary motivation is to see good things come to good people. My goal is to make winners out of every deal and not to take advantage of people. Honesty and trust are also motivating factors.

Q. How did you enter the M&A space?

A. My first M&A experience occurred in the private sector. I had a small role in the first acquisition of a large competitor and the Hart Scott Rodino documentation.

Thereafter, my role grew to be part of the negotiation team on future acquisitions. Another position in the corporate environment involved working with in-house counsel, reviewing documents with in-house counsel, and brainstorming all aspects of agreements for days on end. The brainstorming role played a significant part in my understanding of how important it is to go through each segment of the agreement to understand the contracts completely, as well as what outcomes could arise if someone were to interpret the clause differently.

Q. What advice would you like to provide related to details, terms, and conditions when selling one's business?

A. My best advice is to be very clear as to what you are selling. Describe all assets included in the agreement and define the assets not included. Also, be very clear as to what you are indemnifying and what risks they are assuming. My favored position is to obtain all funds up front and not to extend credit. If selling, try to sell stock as opposed to assets due to the tax benefits. However, there are ways to obtain tax benefits if selling assets, provided the assets are minor when compared to the purchase price. Always engage competent counsel with experience in the M&A field.

Q. Finally, entertain us with an interesting business story.

A. I was the lead in the acquisition of a foreign company. We thought we had the agreement nailed down. The closing was to take place in the law offices of a large firm in a major US city. We flew down the evening before and booked hotel rooms for the night. Closing would take place the next day. When we arrived at the law firm, they had the documents in two languages and all laid out to be signed. The sellers arrived and took the documents to another conference room to read them. They went through both versions to compare and then began renegotiating the entire deal. We had to cancel the bank wire we had planned for the afternoon, and we missed our return flights. Long story short, we finally wired the funds on the afternoon of the third day. Then, the foreigners wanted to celebrate. We could not arrange flights home, so we rented a car and drove back to Michigan.

CHAPTER 10

Differences of Opinion

Differing personalities, backgrounds, ideas, and goals bring a variety of challenges to mergers and acquisitions. In the following pages, we'll look at the generational differences that most often affect M&A transactions. You're probably familiar with the many interesting generational sayings that have been part of the banter through the decades.

Remember the Good Ol' Days?
A grandparent has silver in their hair and gold in their heart.
Study history so you don't repeat the same mistakes.
Today's precious moments are tomorrow's precious memories.

Five Generations affect today's marketplace. Each one is very unique and accomplished in its own right. The characteristics of the various generations aren't always compatible with interactions in family businesses and succession planning.

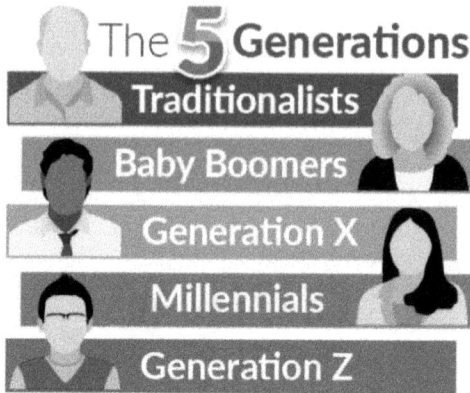

The 5 Generations
Traditionalists
Baby Boomers
Generation X
Millennials
Generation Z

An experienced M&A professional can navigate the differences and find common values to transition ownership and leadership.

Post-War Start-up Businesses

After any war, especially those who engaged in the draft, soldiers returned home to find work. Following World War One, manufacturing jobs opened up for both men and women. Educational training programs, college courses, and government loans for starting a business were offered after World War Two and the Korean and Vietnam wars. The generations that fought in these battles were committed to God, America, and family. This era jump-started entrepreneurial and capitalistic growth in America. Five top characteristics of the Five generations:

Traditionalists (born between 1928 and 1945)

- Quiet
- Patriotism
- Task-oriented

- Sacrifice
- Making ends meet

Boomers (born between 1946 and 1964)

- Professionally accomplished
- Optimistic
- Self Assured
- Goal Oriented
- Relational

Generation X (born between 1965 and 1980)

- Latchkey / Hands off upbringing
- Dressed down / Relaxed look
- Work-Life Balance
- Tech savvy but not tech-dependent
- Independent and often aloof

Millennials (born between 1981 and 1996)

- Transparency
- Collaboration
- Creative
- Diverse and Global Minded
- Fearless

Generation Z (born between 1997 and 2015)

- Success and Money-Driven
- Travel and Adventure

- Well Educated
- Value Family and Societal Improvement
- Digital Natives

With the five distinct generations, you can expect tension, conflict, and arguments due to differing beliefs, attitudes, and values.

When one generation sells to the next, understanding the differences can make for a smoother transition. For instance, we can consider the unique ways people demonstrate respect. The three younger generations we mentioned above tend to treat their children as equals more often, even at a young age. The three older generations appreciate a more definitive show of respect. They come from the "children should be seen and not heard mindset." The incongruent way the generations handle information and view respect can affect succession discussions.

Millennials and Generation Z rely more heavily on family meetings to discuss issues and handle disagreements. They bring their cooperative mindset to the workplace as well. Traditionalists and Baby Boomers operate with the expectation of those who report to them simply following instructions.

The technology gap can also bring stress to the family business. The generations between X and today love the speed, success, and searching power of technology. Prior generations grew up with rotary dial phones and handwritten notes or cards.

Differences in work ethic and educational goals can add stress across generations. Younger generations search for balance in life and like to learn and explore. Older generations focus on being practical and have no idea why the youth want to be permanent students- reading philosophy books vs. a practical, hands-on education.

The younger generations favor autonomy. The older generations never fathomed questioning authority and reciprocally depended on family, friends, and neighbors.

Connecting the Dots to M&A

Your M&A team should be well-versed in the generational issues facing a business being transferred from one generation to another, especially in the formation stage of the process. Certainly, the differences can throw a wrench in negotiations and place stress on all parties.

The differences can cause one generation to place unrealistic expectations on the other generation. Understanding by the M&A team can help them handle the differences well, sometimes with "kid gloves." Negotiations may need a timeout so neither generation loses focus, gets derailed, or threatens to quit.

Dilemma Maxim

When selling your business, honor the differences and hold fast to the commonalities.

$$\$$$

Leaders avoid conflict from time to time. Interestingly, 49 percent of employees identify personalities and egos as the top culprits of business conflict.[5]

$$\$$$

Case Study: Acme Retail Clothing Company

The textile industry started thousands of years ago in the Middle East and Asia. Many of today's silks and fancy fabrics came from these very skilled textile societies.

Fast forward to today; textiles remain in high demand, albeit some younger generations don't appreciate the classics. Their classics are probably jeans, a soft cotton tee shirt with a pocket, and Birkenstock sandals.

Two families welcomed home soldiers after World War Two. Each had an interest in starting a custom men's clothing store.

The community respected these two families and patronized their shop. The veterans sold hundreds of suits, shirts, ties, shoes, etc. They eventually expanded, and each ex-soldier managed and grew a store. Their reputation for impeccable attire flourished to the point they developed another clothing manager and added a third store. Things were rocking.

During their first three decades of success, the soldiers brought in their sons and a daughter too. They divvied up the responsibilities, which served them well for another two decades.

One of the founders wished to retire because of health issues related to serving in the Army. This began the discussion on how to transition his store.

It was much easier to make decisions when it was just the two soldiers. Numerous children added to the mix brought additional opinions and differences. They couldn't agree on the direction of the stores, who was going to run them, or who was a better tailor or buyer of textiles.

The two families got along well, but second-generation egos started to get in the way. Bruised egos are not easy to work with or around.

The families utilized a well-versed business attorney to host the discussions. They hoped to keep the families together and around the table to determine ways to perpetuate the clothing business.

Challenges within the clothing industry from global textile companies and relaxed clothing trends added to the difficulties. The business had been having a hard time adapting, and many points of view developed from the business challenges.

In the end, the lawyer did a good job guiding these families through the business transition of leadership and ownership. However, the families experienced some difficult generation differences, and the attorney wasn't well suited to handle the emotional and psychological issues that happened from time to time.

The clothing store runs under a slightly different business model today. The soldiers started it as a one-stop shop for men. Keeping up with the times, it morphed into a boutique of specialty clothing. Acme Clothing is still profitable, and well-dressed men can be spotted throughout their community.

Interview: Meet Greg McAleenan

Greg and I became friends after our mothers met through a women's Bible study. We clicked right away because we think similarly in the areas of mindset, passion, and servant leadership. He has a unique combination of qualities I admire. He is thoughtful, well-spoken, positive, encourages freely, and believes in the goodness of others.

Q. Share what you learned about business and life growing up and from whom?

A. My dad was a key role model for my siblings and me in business and life. He showed me how to be an entrepreneur and take calculated risks by building and maintaining successful partnerships, primarily in the oil and gas industry. He established a healthy balance of work and family life and illustrated how to hold a strong belief in ourselves and our skills. He gave us this TIP: Always value T - Trust, I - Integrity, and P - Perseverance.

As kids, we noticed Dad's two main sources of success. He lived out a strong faith and picked a fantastic bride to go through all the ups and downs of business and life.

Q. What motivates you as a leader?

A. Although it may sound altruistic or utopian, I derive great satisfaction from seeing others succeed. Achieving goals is extremely rewarding for me and others in the journey of business and life. As my mother preached to us through the years, God's purpose (the why) for my life is to be a servant leader.

Q. How did you enter the M&A space?

A. My family and owning my own business have taught me a great deal about the M&A space. My dad bought a number of companies throughout his career. He acquired one from a family who couldn't get along. My dad offered to help them and bought them out in the end. I quickly learned that some deals go well, others don't. My dad had great success in the oil and gas industry. However, fossil fuels have been on the political chopping block, and technology has changed significantly since Dad got into the business. He had to adjust to the fact that technology accelerates exploration. Each of his pursuits gave me an insight into the M&A arena.

Q. What advice would you like to provide related to the challenges of differing generations when selling one's business and/or transferring leadership?

A. My advice to families passing the baton would be to communicate well, thoroughly, and often. Plus, I can't overemphasize the importance of setting and discussing expectations. They can differ between people, especially during the process of selling. I worked on a deal with an auto racing series where the father wanted to sell to his son. Others advised against it. The father went ahead anyway. The deal imploded because the son didn't have the savvy or skills to run the series like the father had. They lost advertising deals because of the son. The father didn't do his due diligence.

Q. Finally, entertain us with an interesting business story.

A. Here is an interesting story about Bob and Jackie Joyner-Kersee. It's a story about being short-sighted. Mark Rypien Motorsports needed a spokesperson to work with an advertiser for asthma treatment. Most didn't know Jackie suffered from asthma. The drug company wanted Jackie to do a photoshoot with Mark Rypien Motorsports. Bob didn't want her to do the photoshoot if she didn't get paid enough, so the opportunity fell by the wayside.

CHAPTER 11

Huh?

Growing up, my parents corrected me every time I said, "Huh?". Looking back, I realize it probably didn't sound very polite or intelligent. The same applies to business discussions and negotiations. "Huh?" doesn't really convince the audience you are paying attention or value the information they share.

Do you remember playing the telephone game in elementary school? The teacher whispered a descriptive sentence or two, and you had to repeat the details to the person next to you. The sentences continued around the room until the final person revealed what he or she heard. In the end, the sentences ended up being ridiculous and gave a pure lesson on how communication can go terribly wrong.

As an experiment, search online for "effective communication." You will be amazed at the number of hits. People keep writing about it, but the variety of opinions on the right way to share information demonstrates how difficult clear communication is. It may also confirm why we say, "Huh?" a lot.

In a business setting, have you or a co-worker ever been misunderstood? It causes people to become defensive, re-explain themselves, and get a little flush.

Communication Accuracy

Communication studies have shown the main reasons for miscommunication aren't difficult to understand but are hard to correct. Here are a few reasons:

1. **Failure to Listen.** People tend to concentrate on speaking.
2. **Failure to Respect.** People tend to talk down or be blunt.
3. **Failure to Articulate.** The simplest way may be the clearest.
4. **Failure to Express Honestly.** People forget to share feelings as well as facts.
5. **Failure to Compromise.** Don't lower your standards, though.

In an M&A setting, I have experienced all five of the failures of communication. Some corrected more easily than others. Truly Listening is difficult for humans, and respect issues are tough to overcome, especially when working with outside vendors, professionals, and buyers. To articulate, we can restate our position in a different way to be clearer. Honesty becomes problematic because some hide behind their smile or laptop in a meeting. Finally, failure to compromise might be the most difficult issue for business professionals.

Why Compromise?

Whether the discussion of selling your business internally or externally, compromise is expected but isn't naturally embraced. To compromise isn't a sign of weakness or a lesser position. It can be from a win-win vantage point.

In M&A work, it is imperative to consider all options, ideas, tweaks, and changes that occur during the process of succession planning.

What does compromise do to the success of negotiations?

- Compromise allows both sides to feel heard and healthy about the outcome.
- Compromise ensures a peaceful environment and transition.
- Compromise reduces wasted time and prolonged conflict.

Most business owners can agree with and embrace the reasons for a compromise that doesn't require lowered standards, particularly when the goal is succession.

Effective M&A professionals recognize when the negotiations need compromise, often from both parties. As you read the benefits list above, you probably recalled a case or two where compromise was critical to the success of a business sale.

As we wrap up this chapter, let's dive into the differences in pre- and post-sale communication, internal versus external communication, and how a PR firm can help when a wildfire begins to brew.

Pre and Post

An M&A team should provide a foundation of communication for the business owner. The professionals know how and with whom to communicate. The M&A team should be able to guide the owner as he or she decides what and when to share. Obviously, this is important when communicating with the marketplace, but let's focus on the business for now.

Reducing alarm inside the business is key when the topic of transition, succession, and selling the company comes up. The staff, vendors, suppliers, and customers might become curious and wary. Honest communication will bring reassurance in both the pre- and post-sale periods.

The communication you provide inside the company should reflect your culture and emphasize your business legacy. Outside messages need to be a bit more static and straightforward.

When information about mergers and acquisitions gets out prematurely or incorrect rumors prevail, the negative implications for the business can be lasting. The misinformation needs to be smoothed over for a successful sale.

Dilemma Maxim

Good business communications will include elements of promotion and problem-solving. With M&A, you will need both to be successful.

$$\$$$

Business and personal communication is interpreted incorrectly at an embarrassing rate of 75 percent.[6]

$$\$$$

Case Study: Acme Distribution with Foreign Investment Company

A family immigrated to America for a better life. This well-traveled couple had connections in many countries and continents and were scrappers, too.

They started their business small. The father and his three sons handled every aspect of the business from the time the sons were in their early teens. Each member of the family had high expectations regarding work.

The family eventually rented a small warehouse near railroad tracks and not too far from two highways. They started importing household goods, and the business started to take off. They added distribution stores and supplied them with goods. Sales soared.

They added toys, perishables, tools, and more to their inventory. A secondary warehouse helped cut the commute of delivery trucks. Still, they added trucks and drivers. It seemed like whatever they touched turned to gold.

The father and sons continued to forge forward, adding a variety of countries and cultures to their distribution area.

Being sensitive to different languages, meanings, and nuances is important. Education is even more critical. Acme Distribution learned the problem of "Huh?" the hard way.

Some countries they imported from showed an interest in investing in Acme Distribution. Although they experienced frequent communication snafus, The father's strong and almighty response offended a number of key contacts. He told the potential investors, "We don't need any help or your money."

The global suppliers didn't respond very favorably. They joined forces with other suppliers and boycotted shipping to Acme Distribution for one month. This upset the immigrant father, and the sons' attempts to buffer the father's attitude and stubbornness—an act not at all acceptable in their immigrant culture—simply put the sons in hot water with their father.

Communication went awry everywhere–between the company and other countries, the stores they distributed to, and especially among the family.

A family friend was a successful business owner and consultant. He learned of the "Huh?" problem within Acme Distributing and offered to do some coaching. This preceded their hiring of an M&A team.

The coach got the job done. He mended fences and then introduced the idea of inviting outside investors. With business relations healed and inventory starting to flow in and out again, this was the perfect time to look for investors. Everyone seemed open to making better decisions and avoiding costly miscommunication.

Language barriers, time differences, cultural traits, and more created major challenges. The attorneys had to scramble to find bilingual help. They even hired an international consultant.

In the end, the lessons we discussed early in this chapter may have springboarded Acme Distribution to even more success. Outside investment and involvement where it made sense helped the company with expenses and expansion.

Interview: Meet Rob McCarty

Rob and I met a long time ago on a marketing campaign. He and his firm helped one of my companies find a better brand and clearer messaging. He is gifted with creativity, a sound business mind, and tremendous people skills.

Q. Share what you learned about business and life growing up and from whom?

A. Great question. I learned a lot about how to act as an adult from my Grandpa. He was a union steward after serving in the Army during WW2. He taught me a lot about how to treat people through his example. He was calm, smart, and caring. In my own business life, I've learned so much by working with such a wide range of leaders and entrepreneurs, mentors, and others. I believe if you are paying attention, you can glean a great deal of information simply by how people act, react, and convey; simply stated, every moment is a moment to grow. I've learned how businesses function, and in many cases, I figured out how to discern real problems, marketing or otherwise, and how to address them.

Q. What motivates you as a leader?

A. Helping people—my team, clients, and family—equals my motivation. I want to do nothing more than to leave someone or something in a better place than where I found it.

Q. How did you enter the M&A space?

A. A number of my clients have transitioned leadership and ownership. As a marketer, I primarily strategized rolling out messages around M&A for sellers and buyers. A number of the transactions involved working with PR services to minimize rumors and damaging gossip that can easily occur about a business owner selling his or her company.

Q. What advice would you like to provide related to communication, public relations, and messaging when selling your business?

A. Communication can be a delicate dance. You need to ask yourself questions like, who will this affect? When do they need to hear it, and from whom? Will the message provide assurance and hope for continuity or improvement? You need to consider all your audiences—family, leadership, staff, vendors, suppliers, consumers, customers, etc. While there is no perfect science here, the goal is to create a smooth transition. We like to say when we do our best work, it goes unnoticed and makes the seller or buyer look like they've done it a thousand times. Most people have no idea we are working behind the scenes.

Q. Finally, entertain us with an interesting business story.

A. I once worked for a CEO who controlled a portfolio of about forty companies. We were navigating some branding elements for one of those entities, and I said, "I'm just not sure this is there yet," though I couldn't articulate what was bothering me. In the kindest words, he said, "Rob, I want to introduce you to the 98% rule." okay, what is that? "Well, in most things, when we get to 98%, it's better than good enough. It's likely great!" He continued, "The final 2% we need to reach perfection for most practices is the most expensive and yields the least in terms of return unless you are working in literal finance, investing, or math. Anything that can be considered subjective means perfection is impossible, and trying to achieve it will drive you mad. 98 percent will be good enough for most applications. You'll save time, resources, and frustration. You will truly move things forward, better and faster for the majority of the people you serve.

CHAPTER 12

When the Applause Ceases

Everyone enjoys a bit of applause, and being in the "the buck stops here" position for years has given you the chance to receive those accolades. People must go through you to make a decision or get things done. When you lead a meeting, all eyes are on you. Your business card states President, Founder, CEO, or Chair.

Customers, vendors, and industry leaders know you are the person they need to meet with to get an endorsement or join your network. This isn't bad. It comes with owning a business. Society holds a business owner in a higher level of esteem.

When one decides to sell, the applause will eventually cease. This can be scary for the owner after so many years of being in the middle of the action. Selling your business isn't the end of the story, though. In 2008, business leader Bob Buford wrote *Half Time*, a compelling book on life and retirement. In this book, Bob reveals the perils of a mid-life crisis that can happen to fellow leaders, and he challenges his readers to find purpose and meaning in the second half.

Most business owners started or purchased their businesses. They take great pride in what they've grown. The owners put blood, sweat, and tears into their companies. They sometimes refer to the business as their baby. They birthed it, invested in it, grew it, and matured it. It brings them pride.

Retiring and selling is difficult., We see it often in entertainment and sports. An athlete keeps going because the game and the crowd intoxicate them. Performers well into their 70s or 80s can't sing from their diaphragm like they used to. They lack the energy needed for three-hour concerts. Still, you'll find them in casinos and lounges instead of packed concert halls.

A business owner goes through similar concerns and worries. They may even face a similar level of anxiety. What will it be like? Will anyone stay in touch? What am I without my company?

As an M&A professional, hone your skills to recognize anxiety surrounding a leader or owner's fear of transitioning into what they see as irrelevancy. Anxiety can be paralyzing. It can change a person. Succession planning and selling isn't just about the numbers. The "soft tissue" areas are critical to a happy sale and healthy transition.

What is Soft Tissue?

The "soft tissue" of mergers and acquisitions refers to the psychological or emotional element of a business. Examples of soft tissue could be:

- The owner's spouse worries the sale will ruin the family and just wants good Easters and Christmases.
- One team member feels slighted because they thought they were the heir apparent. Many times, rescuing this relationship helps tremendously in the transition.
- Concerns, hopes, and dreams make up a good bit of soft tissue items. We can help by finding out how many of these they would like to or prefer not to share publicly.
- The owner's exit plan is a critical soft tissue element. It's why the M&A team was hired—to help them sell well.

Uncertainty

Type "A" personalities feel most comfortable when they can control everything. However, as much as they try, we know it's tough, if not impossible. The uncertainty that lies in M&A and the fear of the fact it might not work out drives Type As to worry and strive.

Scientifically, anxiety causes havoc with brain health. Uncertainty is an elicitor and modulator of emotions, even in business owners. When uncertainty hangs in the air, the brain requires extra energy to make sense of things. This manifests into anxiety. One of the main impacts of uncertainty is doubt. It takes over the mind and makes it difficult to think well and clearly.

Though many say worry is a waste of time, humans sure do worry a lot. For the owner selling their business, worry is common. The M&A team can certainly give assurances and help reduce the worry and anxiety in this rewarding business process—succession planning.

Similar to piloting a plane, taking off in business is easier than landing softly. Starting a company isn't easy, but it is easier than selling. Most owners will sell only one business in their lifetime. Some outliers have bought and sold several; however, since most haven't experienced a merger or acquisition before, we can understand why they would benefit from a solid M&A team to journey with. The owner may have hobbies or outside interests they want to pursue. Some might even wish to start a different business. A few go through a process to reinvent themselves. The M&A team can assist with exit planning and help the owner land on both feet.

The experienced team of professionals will be able to map out the future and clear the path for the business owner to sell well and exit with his head held high. Many owners think they can travel for the next twenty years and not get bored. Some think golfing or fishing every day would be heavenly. Whatever the leader chooses, it's important to remember God created us to move, labor, and have relationships. We are meant for more than sitting in a rocking chair on a porch up north in the mountains, letting nature's quiet soothe us.

Silence

When the applause ceases, the silence can be deafening. For some business leaders, leaving the habits and routines of the pace of business with its many moving parts can feel stressful.

When you sell and maybe retire, you'll have to adjust to the pace and lack of demands. It can be hard to get used to. Some people hate silence—the scientific term is a sedate phobia.

Dilemma Maxim

Next! After the sale, an owner will need time and counsel to really find their second half.

$$

Business owners self-reported that anxiety and depression go up 40 percent after they sell.[7]

$$

Case Study: Acme Professional Sports Company

Athletes tend to hang on too long, and their careers whimper in the end.

- Joe Namath was cut by NFL Champions New York Jets and struggled to play one season for the LA Rams.
- Chris Chelios was a hockey workhorse. He played a valuable role for venerable teams like Montreal, Chicago, and Detroit. His play ended up slipping poorly on the ice—not scoring a single goal with the Atlanta Thrashers.
- Even Michael Jordan lands on this list. After six rings in Chicago, the team sort of broke up, but Mike yearned to keep playing with the Wizards. There, he did not have his best games.
- Others who kept playing but not well were Joe Montana, Brett Favre, and even GOAT boxer Roy

Jones Jr., who ended his career with multiple losses by knockout in a row.

Acme Baseball, a minor league baseball team, was started by numerous business people in a small eastern shoreline community. Professional baseball was new to the community. The excitement and attendance skyrocketed. The park was family-friendly. Really good MLB prospects came out of Acme Baseball.

Success continued. They adapted and offered more contests to the fans. With new players, new uniforms, and more championships, it seemed like the wins would continue.

Acme Baseball became the talk of professional baseball. People traveled to the quaint town to try to emulate their success.

The leadership group for the team was extremely solid, competent, creative, and fun. This went a long way to building a valuable franchise.

The founders were getting older and considered tapering off and handing the baton to the next leadership group. The conversations went well. The transition was announced, and confidence in the franchise remained solid. The MLB was thrilled that the baton had passed well.

The two founding partners had a beautiful community send off into retirement. Really, it included fond appreciation for all they had done in bringing baseball to their town.

Months later, after the season, the partners experienced the quietness of moving on, and the organization continued successfully. Their phone didn't ring. Their email box is never filled. People didn't reach out to them like before. The silence was deafening.

Years later, one partner found other things that excited him and used his talents. Nothing was as exciting as running the baseball team. But he figured it out.

The other partner fell into despair because the applause ceased.

Interview: Meet John Hendrickson

John and I have known each other since Little League. John went on to study at the University of Michigan and enjoyed an exciting career at Perrigo, a global pharmaceutical manufacturer and distributor. He held many leadership roles, lastly serving as President. His insights on M&A will definitely be enlightening.

Q. Share what you learned about business and life growing up and from whom?

A. My parents (Dad was a teacher and coach. Mom was stay-at-home and very engaged with us kids) held high standards even though we weren't well off. Still, we were a hard-working grassroots family. They modeled achievement, aiming high, respect for others, and integrity in your words and handshakes. I had three important mentors in my career too. Ralph Klingenmeyer taught me not to overthink and trust my instincts. Dick Hanson showed me to attack the problem and deal with things directly. Finally, Mike Jandernoa was a thought leader who pulled people together to accomplish big things.

Q. What motivates you as a leader?

A. Wired to compete, I enjoy the battle, the grind. I love to compete and win with others. To me, leadership is about establishing and developing a strong team.

Q. How did you enter the M&A space?

A. I have had the privilege of working on over fifty acquisitions in my career. The acquisitions range from five figures to multiple billions. Many deals worked out very well, some not so well. What we learned was that people and culture played a big part in those cases where things didn't go as well as we had hoped. After all the due diligence and multiple eyes on the details and docs for a deal, we were about 80% successful.

Q. What advice would you like to provide related to exiting and transitioning from owning a business to retirement when selling one's business?

A. Having witnessed a number of leaders and owners exit, my advice is to stay engaged and keep growing. Slowing from 100 mph to a crawl isn't healthy for a driven leader.

Q. Finally, entertain us with an interesting business story.

A. We acquired a very large manufacturer, and things moved along well. Closing was seamless. We took a handful of our execs to meet with their entire organization and share our excitement and expectations for the merger. When the event was about to begin, the owner was nowhere to be found. As we addressed the large crowd of employees, the owner barged in the back door and made his way to the podium. He started with, "You will be in good hands. Thanks for all you did. I am headed to Vegas to shop for Ferraris." He then turned to me and said, "It's all yours," as he walked out of the meeting room, grabbing a fake fern and tucking it under his arm. We never heard from him again. Obviously, he was ready to retire and spend his new money.

BONUS CHAPTER 13

Leading Well, Finishing Well

Owning a business takes many skills and talents, plus it requires an owner to be intentional and sacrificial. Many authors, books, and articles have been written about leadership. You can learn from leaders in many formats.

Calculated risks are necessary for success. True leaders serve rather than dictate. You'll find many leadership lessons along the business ownership journey if you look for them.

Leaving a legacy is important, especially if the owner started a family-owned business. Sure, the original owner feels a sense of pride, but he or she also has a passion to leave it well in the hands of the next generation.

A growing business develops others. By duplicating your leadership, you create both an offensive plan for your business as well as a defensive.

Building a bullpen prevents your legacy business from floundering—not only after your retirement but also while you're vacationing or recovering from surgery. Establishing a coaching and mentoring program in your legacy business is a smart offering. The growth of the individual must be motivational and measurable.

Below, you'll find ten top authors who have provided resources to help business owners throughout their careers.

Deb Boelkes
Brendon Burchard
Jim Collins
Stephen Covey
Hans Finzel
Marshall Goldsmith

James Kouzes & Barry Posner
Patrick Lencioni
John Maxwell
Simon Sinek

Dilemma Maxim

Owning a business has many perks. Leading a business has many responsibilities and rewards. Stewarding a business is the ultimate duty. Start well and finish well—the perfect "bookends" to your business ownership journey.

Interview: Meet Nick Adamy

Nick and I were introduced by fellow M&A pros. Plus, Nick's firm, Adamy Valuation, has advised and completed valuations for clients of mine. Nick is an expert in the truest sense. Whether developing a valuation for a business client in the marketplace or explaining/testifying for a client in a dispute, Nick is the consummate professional.

Q. Share what you learned about business and life growing up and from whom?

A. Father presented very good business traits to me. I observed and worked alongside him. He was an exquisite business relationship builder. A fabulous networker, he found common ground and genuineness with others he met. Early in my valuation career, working for a large national firm, I witnessed several great examples of integrity in action. In one memorable example, a Managing Director and I were in a meeting in New York City surrounded by high-power Wall Street attorneys and investment bankers. We attended on behalf of the employees in a complex restructuring, and we were the last obstacle to closing a deal. Under tremendous pressure to rubber-stamp the deal, my MD held out until he could get terms we believed were fair to the employees, to the chagrin of the bankers and lawyers.

Q. What motivates you as a leader?

A. I find building something worthwhile with teammates and their talents rewarding as a leader. The younger generations fascinate me. Accomplishing important objectives with a team gives me the best feeling. Tying this to business owners, I get satisfaction when I can help them successfully navigate their ownership transition.

Q. How did you enter the M&A space?

A. I have a background in engineering, and I love building things. This drove me to build the valuation practice my father had begun. I am fortunate and grateful for the large head start he gave me by creating a successful practice. I went to grad school for finance and then transitioned to a valuation with a large national firm before joining my father. I am privileged to have seen and learned so much.

Q. What advice would you like to share related to valuation, exiting, and transitioning from one's leadership and ownership?

A. Transactions garner a lot of attention related to finances, figures, and facts. I would advise owners to heavily consider the emotional side of M&A. The human element is almost always more important than financial details.

Plenty of deals have been secured or sunk because of this aspect.. Numbers don't lie, but humanity sure can trip things up in the process. The three areas I turn to in M&A deals are family dynamics, organizational health, and culture.

Q. Finally, entertain us with an interesting business story.

A. I was one of the advisors involved in a bitter shareholder dispute among siblings in a family business that dragged on for several years. Failed mediations and growing tension Made the dispute become the tail that wagged the dog. After multiple mediation attempts, a fresh set of eyes made an insightful finding. The holdout sibling, who had refused all settlement offers to date, was not making the decisions. The mediator realized his wife really called the shots. Even though she did not own the shares, she had tremendous influence over her husband. The mediator got the spouse on the phone, updated her on the facts of the situation, and the deal was done. It was insightful to recognize the subtle dynamics behind this sibling's apparent stubbornness. It turned out they had been ignoring the key decision-maker.

Endnotes

[1] Guta, Michael. Small Business Trends. "75% of Struggling Small Business Owners Believe Being Disorganized Leads to Productivity Loss." June 7, 2023. https://smallbiztrends.com/being-disorganized-leads-to-productivity-loss/

[2] SeeKen, "Types of Frustration," SeeKen.org, July 11, 2018, https://seeken.org/types-of-frustration/.

[3] Daugherty, Greg. Investopedia. "What Is Quiet Quitting—and Is It a Real Trend?" March 8, 2024. https://www.investopedia.com/what-is-quiet-quitting-6743910.

[4] Danielle Mcleod, "The Devil Is in the Details - Origin & Meaning," GRAMMARIST, January 20, 2023, https://grammarist.com/words/devil-is-in-the-details-vs-god-is-in-the-detail/.

[5] Lindner, Jannik. Gitnux. "Must-Know Workplace Conflict Statistics." Updated December 23, 2023. https://gitnux.org/workplace-conflict-statistics/.

6   Saylor Dotorg Github. "The Power of Selling."
    Accessed April 25, 2024. https://saylordotorg.github.
    io/text_the-power-of-selling/s08-01-ready-set-
    communicate.html

7   Sahlgreen, Gabriel H. IEA 50 "Work Longer, Live
    Healthier." May 2013. https://www.iea.org.uk/wp-content/
    uploads/2016/07/Work%20Longer,%20Live_Healthier.pdf

About the Author

Greg Heeres is a best-selling author of five books on customer service, creativity, leadership, and succession planning. He is described as a sales champion, M&A navigator, and leadership rascal. As an advisor, problem solver, professional storyteller, and popular presenter, Greg Heeres's passion is to instruct and inspire organizations and leaders to reach their maximum potential.

For over 20 years, he has provided high-quality training and high-level coaching to maximize sales and develop leadership teams at businesses from entrepreneurial start-ups to Fortune 500 companies such as AT&T, Chevron, and Hartford.

Aside from speaking on sales excellence and succession planning and having extensive experience with succession planning and business M&A transactions, Greg is a high performer in sports, business, and life.

CONNECT WITH GREG

Follow him on your favorite social media platforms today.

INTERESTED IN HEARING MORE FROM GREG?
INQUIRE TO HAVE HIM SPEAK AT YOUR NEXT EVENT
Visit maximizeleadership.com/speaking